Your First Job

How to make a success of starting work and ensure your first years are the launch of a successful career

Mark Blayney

D1471880

www.theworkpress.com

The Work Press

www.theworkpress.com

Your First Job

How to make a success of starting work and ensure your first years are the launch of a successful career

*A number of books and sources of information are referred to during the course of this guide. For online links to many of these visit www.theworkpress.com.

1   Why you and why this book?

Congratulations on starting your first job.

You'll probably experience a honeymoon period for your first few days where everybody will be nice and friendly as they show you around, introduce you to people and welcome you on board.

Even so it's going to feel a bit odd. After all you've just left a place, whether it's school, college or university where not only did you know your way around since you'd been there for a number of years, but where (leaving aside the teaching staff) you'd been in a relatively senior position, and surrounded by people that you've grown to know over a prolonged period. Whereas now you're starting somewhere completely new, with its own rules and networks that you're going to need to get used to, as probably the most junior member of staff, knowing precisely no one.

By the end of week two, with piles of work landing on you apparently at random, from people who seem demanding and who expect you to just know what to do with it all, and the phone going all the time, you might feel yourself drowning as you wonder how you are ever going to handle it all.

Well the first thing to say is that you're not alone in going through this.

Schools or colleges are great at getting you the qualifications you need to land a job and guiding you in how to apply and land it. But given the many different career paths for students, it can be difficult for them to fully prepare you for the range of practical issues you will run into at work and how to make a success of it once you've started.

And that's a pity, because it's an important formative experience. Your first 'proper' job is potentially the foundation for what you are going to be doing for the next 40 or 50 years, and how far you are going to get, so if you want to have a great career it's important to make a great start, and it's never too early to begin either.

If you learn just one lesson from this book, please let it be about taking charge of your own working future: **Don't just work in your job, work on it**.

As you go through the book hopefully the second will be: **It's all**

about having successful respectful relationships with people.

And if you learn a third, **Your boss is your customer, find out what your boss really wants, and then give it to them,** then you will really be on your way to a successful working life.

Work is a complex place and a complex set of relationships

Becoming employed for the first time, particularly in a large organisation, whether in the private or public sector, you may have an expectation that the world of work is going to operate something like this:

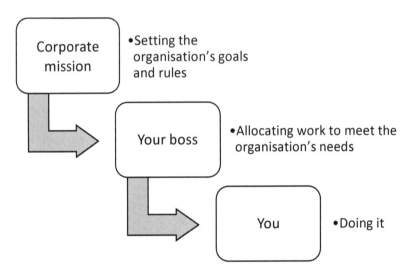

What you probably imagine

Unfortunately, it's a lot more complicated than that. This is real life; you are mingling with real people and they will all have their own real interests and priorities; you are actually in the centre of a net of interlocking interests and priorities.

What you'll actually find is probably more like this:

What you are really in

Yes, corporate headquarters somewhere may have a grand plan, but your local branch, division or department will have its own interests and agenda which may or may not interlock well with the corporate strategy (anything from *Hey, let's organise things so the big boys can't suddenly decide to off-shore our jobs*, to sales hating production, and vice versa, or 'suits' and 'support staff' living in seemingly different worlds).

In all this your boss (and theirs) will also have their own agenda, whether it's an ambitious desire to climb the greasy pole, or a simple desire to keep their head down and serve out their time to retirement without rocking the boat.

And then there are all the people you work with, each with their own desires, demands, dreams and agendas, none of which they park at the door when they arrive in the morning.

And in the middle of all this?

You.

Yep, sorry, life at work is complicated. Get used to it.

And that goes for whether you are in the public or private sector. My career has been in business so when writing I'll tend to be assuming that you have joined a commercial organisation and most of my examples will come from this type of environment. But as I hope you'll already see, the issues you need to deal with in the world of work are first and foremost about people, so the chapters in this book will apply wherever you are going to work.

Oh, and by the way, all those company rules and that handbook and organisation chart they gave you on induction day?

They don't tell you half the story. The way any organisation runs is actually down to its culture which is the way people think, and act, the acceptable norms of behaviour and the way *'we do things here'*, little of which is ever written down and all of which you are going to need to pick up and learn on the job, pretty quickly, if you are to be accepted and make a success of things.

The good news? This book is here to help.

Chapter 2 is a crash course on a few essentials intended to ensure you get off on the right foot so I suggest you concentrate on these key things in your first month or so.

The rest of the book is your guide to managing.

You didn't realise you were being recruited as a manager?

Well you were. Whatever level you start at, very soon you're going to be expected to manage yourself, your time and your work, your communications, your relationships with those around you, and even your boss.

At the same time, for your own sake you are going to have to look to manage both your career and the sorts of emotional and stress issues you come across in the world of work.

So your management training starts here.

And good luck, wherever you take your career.

2 Managing first impressions

They say you never get a second chance to make a first impression (actually if you think about it that's complete rubbish, you just have to make it on someone else, somewhere else), so this chapter is focused on making those crucial first impressions in those critical first few weeks at work.

It's therefore a bit of a catch-all of some basic information and survival tips, a mix of Dos and Don'ts to get you started.

Many of these things are a foretaste of subjects we'll be coming back to and looking at in more depth in later chapters so don't worry too much at this stage if you find yourself thinking, *Fine but how do I actually do that?*

Key behaviours – the Dos

There are a limited number of things you probably need to concentrate on in your first month or so as summarised below.

- **Be there and be there on time** – one of the simplest steps you can take, but one which is entirely within your control and which is very visible and gets noticed, is to be punctual. Downstream in your career you may need to deal with the cultural problems of presenteeism but don't worry about this now.

   At this stage of your career you want to be building social capital and this is one of the quickest first steps to doing so.

   So you should always arrive early (*on time is late*, some say) and crucially stay on for as long as there seems to be work to do (never be the first to leave).

   You will probably come across people at some point in your career who always spend the last quarter of an hour before the end of the official working day packing up so they can get away on the dot every time. Clock-watcher is the term and it's not a description you want to pick up.

   One tip I've seen is if asked why you are there you can say; *I just want to be available to help out with anything that needs doing and learn as much as I can.*

- **Get your game face on, give a good impression from the moment you walk in** – if you've seen the film *Pulp Fiction*, think about how Vincent and Jules go about getting into character outside the door of the flat they are about to hit. They are heading into their own particular work environment so they deliberately adopt their work personas before starting.

  One of my colleagues on a turnaround had a checklist he kept in his car and went through every morning before he walked into the office; reminding himself he was there as a director, staff would be looking to him for leadership, and he had to conduct himself confidently, smile and be upbeat.

  So, develop something similar for yourself. Don't just walk in to your work in the morning. Before you get there deliberately make a little time every morning to think about how to give the best impression from the moment you arrive, and if nothing else, before you walk in the door, smile!

- **Dress appropriately** – this could reasonably fit as part of giving a good impression but it's important that you and your appearance fit in with the organisation's culture and values. A professional firm will have certain standards of professional dress code which can either be quite proscriptive (one financial organisation I'm told issued a formal dress code notice stating in effect, 'No cleavage, anywhere, from anyone') or simply enforced through the cultural norms. Look around at what everyone else is wearing and check that your dress is appropriate.

  Not being too slack (you have flip flops on while everyone else around you in your law office is in a suit and tie) is the obvious failing, but sometimes being overdressed (everyone else in your software firm is in beachwear while you have a three-piece suit and gleamingly polished shoes) can be a problem in achieving a cultural fit with your colleagues.

  Of course, dress can also vary depending on the role people have to fulfil, so while the coders at that software firm might work in very casual clothes, the sales staff who are out selling services into big corporates will have to dress formally to give the right professional image to the clients, ie fit in with that culture.

- **Listen and take notes** – quite simply **write** everything down.

Your work is going to be overwhelming to start with and people will be telling you lots of different things, which you'll be expected to remember.

If you don't write it down, you won't remember. There'll just be too much to absorb too quickly.

So, write it down!

Get yourself a notebook (or the App you prefer) and carry it with you everywhere you go at work. Use it to note down everything: work to do, names (and contact details), deadlines, ideas, everything. It's important to realise how much you are in learning mode in these early days and how much you are therefore going to need to take notes to be able to refer back.

Immediately this will help you keep yourself organised and avoid forgetting things that need doing, people you need to deal with and so on (at one UK business I've heard about, being seen without a notebook is regarded as a disciplinary offence!).

Longer term it will help you as well. People are usually very willing to help someone new and show them the ropes, but there are few things more irritating than finding they have to be told again and again. No one wants to have to go through telling you the same stuff twice or three times and this will quickly infuriate them, not least because it shows a lack of respect for their time and the effort they've already made for you.

Whereas if you can acquire the reputation that you only have to be told once (because you write it down and learn it) then you will be earning credibility and a good reputation.

- **Plan** – a properly organised and prioritised To Do list is your best friend. It's the way you order and organise your world and turn the stream of work heading your way into something manageable (a subject covered in more detail in Chapter 4).

The truth is, if you don't plan, others will plan for you and you will simply end up reacting to and running around after their priorities, not yours.

To begin with you simply need to start daily planning for yourself. For the moment, at the end of each day sit back for a moment and take the time to put together an outline plan of what's expected of you tomorrow. In your notebook, you'll be keeping a schedule of all the dates when projects are due or expected so you can keep track of them and pull them into your To Do list for the next day. If having a structured format for writing down notes, planning your day and prioritising your projects would help then use a copy of *My Time and Project Manager* (see the section on further reading and resources).

As part of this process go through today's list to make sure you've done what you were supposed to do and to carry over anything that didn't get finished today into tomorrow's list.

- **Work to make everyone else around you look good** – forget about yourself for the moment and instead work on the basis that your job is simply to make your boss (and your team of co-workers) look good (much more on this in Chapter 5).

  Try to think about what their goals are and how you can support them. Ask yourself:

  o   What does your boss want and why?

  o   And so, what you can do to help them so you become their, and your team's, go to person for getting things done.

  Be proactive and always look for chances to help and be useful. This will make you stand out and in due course you'll start to be seen as indispensable.

  If you focus on serving others what you are actually doing is investing in your social capital, while at the same time helping yourself to learn and develop. Do this throughout your career and it will pay back handsomely, believe me.

- **Always be ready to learn** – start off by being honest and embracing the fact you are new. No one expects you to have all the answers so don't pretend you do because it's not going to fool anyone.

  Instead treat your job as a chance to learn, but don't simply expect to sit back and be taught.

  You need to be proactive and self-starting. So, if you find a problem, don't just go running for help immediately or ask someone to show you what to do. Instead think about the issue to see if you can come up with answers or options yourself, and then if you need to, go and check you have got the right answer.

Don't be afraid to ask for help. Yes, as we've covered above you don't want to be bothering people for the same instruction time after time, but if you have a problem you can't solve or aren't sure you have the right answer for, then ask.

I'll let you into a secret, people generally like to be asked for help. It makes them feel good about themselves (*I'm seen and respected as an expert*) and what they're doing (*I'm being nice and helpful, how great am I?*) and if they're passionate about what they do they will positively want to share their knowledge with you. Some of them will even write a book about it...

And while we're on the subject of learning, learn through errors. Cock-ups and errors happen to us all, it's part of life. When you make a mistake admit it, don't hide it. Take it to your boss (yes, you read that right) and show them what you've done and why. Work out together what needs to be done to fix it and how you can avoid it in future.

Trust me, it's a better way than them finding out for themselves down the line.

- **Think about what you are doing and why**. Your firm is employing your brain as well as your hands. Early on in my career I had to prepare what were known as Section 48 reports on companies, which I did the way everyone else did in my department. I found an old one to use as a template, and in those days actually cut and pasted the details of the current company onto it to be typed up.

  Or I did until I got a new boss who called me into his office, threw my report at me and chewed me out asking me why my Section 48 report didn't meet the requirements of Section 48 of the relevant law? To which the answer was, although I didn't say so at the time, because:

  o I'd never read Section 48 of the relevant act, even though I knew it existed; because

  o It had never even occurred to me that I ought to so as to

check I knew what I was doing!

Instead I'd simply had my brain parked in a bucket by the side of my desk while I got on with pushing my papers.

And as your career develops make sure you continue to learn. Take responsibility for your own development. After the bollocking I got from my boss for that report I realised I needed technical training in the area I was working in, so I signed up for a professional training course which eventually gave me my next business qualification.

- **Seek feedback** – check in with your manager on a regular basis to get their view on how you are doing. Your job is to make them look good, so don't you want to know if they feel you have?

  Share your To Do list with them at the start of each day, is it covering everything they need or is there anything else they want? This helps you ensure you get off on the right track and shows them you are being proactive in planning your work.

  Check in with them before you go home to ensure everything's been covered off that's needed today.

  Show them your notes on a regular basis (that in itself is likely to impress them). Ask them whether they feel things have gone right and whether there's anything you could have done better?

  If there is, then look to make sure you do it next day.

  Depending on how formal your workplace is, you might seek a regular feedback session, say on a monthly basis (particularly while you are working towards the end of your probation period). If you can get this agreed pull together a short summary from your notes about what you've been doing, what you've learnt, and what you see the key tasks and areas for development are for the next month.

  In essence, this is some of the material a decent appraisal and development system should be requiring on a six-monthly or annual basis for all staff, you are just engaging in the same sort of process on an accelerated basis during your first few months when your need for development is likely to be most acute.

- **Participate** – your work is a social environment and to be successful you need to understand the culture and build relationships. There is something to learn from each of the people around you, so dive on in and become part of the team.

What's the coffee making rota? (Probably you as the newbie, but you never know.)

Where do people go for lunch? Go with them and talk to people.

Same again after work if people socialise.

- **Work out the social rules, quickly** – every workplace will have its own little customs and practises which are the social norms everybody knows, works by and unconsciously expects everybody else to follow. So, if you don't, because nobody told you or showed you, then people will see you (probably unfairly but there you go) as acting anti-socially.

   Just getting a cup of coffee can be a minefield. What's the fridge and milk etiquette? Do people make a round of hot drinks, or get their own? Do people have their own mugs or is it a free for all? If you've used the last of the water in the kettle are you expected to fill it up again? What happens to dirty cups? Are you expected to wash up after yourself, put them in a dishwasher or leave them for a cleaner?

   Get this wrong and you'll be seen as the one who took my mug (and my milk), didn't make a round of drinks for everyone, left the kettle empty for the next person and left your dirty cups in the sink as a mess for someone else to have to wash up and put away.

- **Don't burnout in month one** – the first point on this list was about being in early and staying on while there's work to do. But this needs to be tempered with looking after yourself, since taken to extremes there's always more work to do and you could then get sucked into working longer and longer hours.

   Unfortunately, in the work environment there's always more work, and there'll always be some people who will be happy to let you put in all the hours (even though in the long run this will lead to stress and lower productivity), the only person you can really trust to look out for you, is you.

You need to take responsibility for your own work-life balance right from the start.

You need to decide what your boundaries are. You need to ensure that you keep a life outside of work and you need to make sure you work hours you are comfortable with and take the holidays and breaks you need.

The Don'ts

If those are the Dos, then there are also clearly some Don'ts that you want to avoid.

Some of these are obviously the flip side of the Dos. If looking business-like and presentable is a Do, then turning up looking like a slacker or a tramp (in either UK or US meanings) are obviously a no-no.

The other key Don'ts are probably also pretty obvious if you stop to think, the only problem being that sometimes people don't:

- **Getting drunk when socialising** – if there are social activities organised at or around work then you ought to be taking advantage of these to meet your colleagues outside the work environment. It can be a great shortcut towards getting to know them and building good relationships. But remember, this is now work and you're an employee and not a student anymore so don't let a free bar go to your head.

  Enjoy yourself. Yes, you want to get on with people and make a good impression. Fun, good company and sensible is good, beneficial even, given that as you get on in your career socialising is likely to become an ever more important part of it at senior levels (see Chapter 8) and these skills are seen as an asset.

  But whether there's actually a manager there or not, be careful in what you do and how you behave so don't overdo it, as stories about you will get around and get back to the office quicker than you can ever imagine. An outrageous drunken clown is not an asset, they're a business liability.

- **Gossip/over confide** – neither your manager, nor your co-worker are your best friend (certainly not yet anyway).

  So, don't gossip about what you think about other people in the workplace, who you like and who you don't, or over confide about issues at home. All that's going to do is lead to trouble as it gets around the grapevine and you don't want to be seen to be a source of trouble, do you? Thought not.

- **Grandstanding your personal views** – following on from above, you will probably share a range of views amongst your friends where there's a degree of consensus or acceptance of differing points of view on anything from politics to football teams. But that's amongst a self-selecting group of people (as anyone with, say, political views that were completely unacceptable to the rest of the group is, in practise, unlikely to stay a member of that group for long).

But the people you work with aren't brought together because they like each other's company and share each other's outlooks and opinions. They are all there simply because they were hired to do jobs which needed doing, so you need to appreciate:

  - there is likely to be a wide range of deeply held views in your workplace, some of which you may fundamentally disagree with; and

  - the last thing your employer wants is someone starting arguments with other employees, particularly over non-work related issues.

All of which is a long-winded way of saying remember you are there to work, not debate or campaign, so park your politics or whatever at the door and don't bring up contentious subjects at work, certainly not until you have a thorough understanding of the culture, and have established strong and respected relationships that can take the weight of your opinions.

Starting conflict in the workplace is not the way to give your boss what they want.

- **Never forget you are now representing your organisation** – your employer is hiring you and certain of your attributes to do a job. Your private life is your private life and while it's up to you how you live it, it's not unreasonable for your employer to expect that what you make publicly available shouldn't bring the organisation into disrepute.

This is an area where I'd expect quite a lot of potential conflict to arise in employer/employee relationships, particularly as social norms change. (How many years back would it have been when there could have been concerns about employees coming out as gay, for example?)

However, without getting into a debate about the rights and wrongs of it, the advice simply needs to be, in these days of ubiquitous social media, think very carefully about what image you are conveying. These days what happens in Vegas stays on Facebook, Twitter, Tumblr, Pinterest, Instagram...

- **Use social media/gaming at work** – your employer is likely to have the old-fashioned idea that they've actually hired you to work. Unless that work is to create a viral social media buzz, then you are not there to chat to your mates, work on your high score, scroll your Facebook feed, download pirated movies, or curate your blog. That's all personal stuff so keep it for personal time (apart from pirating stuff aka the theft of copyright material that someone has slaved over creating – just don't do that at all).

Some practicalities

It's also worth covering some practicalities that should be sorted out in your first few days on the job, and if not you might want to speak to your Human Resources (HR) or Personnel Department to ensure these are organised:

- **Employment contract and terms and conditions** – you will need to be issued with and sign a written contract of employment specifying the key terms of your employment such as your job title, who you report to, your rate of pay, hours, place of work, and holiday entitlement.

  It should also specify the details of any initial **probation period** so you are clear on the length and review date. You should also make sure you understand as far as possible what your probationary period will be judged on (and if there any formal targets, for example) so you can focus on what you need in order to ensure success at that stage.

- **Employee handbook** – the employment contract is usually quite a short agreement and it will often include a reference to an employee handbook which is a much larger set of documents, which may be annotated and updated over time. The handbook is where details of the organisation's policies, rules, codes of conduct, and key employment processes such as appraisal systems, grievance procedures and disciplinary processes are set out.

While almost all organisations have one of these, they vary widely in how it is used and viewed. Broadly the larger and more formally organised the organisation, the more this will be used and referred to as a day to day management tool and so you need to be aware of it and its key provisions.

At the other end of the scale smaller and less formally managed organisations may have compiled one once (or had their solicitors write one when they last updated their employment contracts) but it's sitting gathering dust in a cupboard somewhere as no one ever looks at it, much less updates it. In which case the advice is probably leave well alone.

- **Job specification** – as you've been hired to do a job, it's useful if it's spelled out what that job is as a first step in giving you a fighting chance of understanding it and doing it.

  However, please never, ever, think that your job description is the be all and end all of what you are there to do. Think of it as the minimum core of what you must do, and then start looking at what else you can do on top of it.

  Never even think, let alone say, That's not in my job description. No one likes a jobsworth.

- **Induction** – most organisations of any size should have some form of induction process as a way of bringing new staff on board. The degree of formality will vary enormously and can range from a simple tour and introductory checklists, through to formal training and issuing of copies of mission statements and charters of How we work with each other.

  At the very least you should expect briefings on basics such as Health and Safety policies and procedures and usually IT and security; as well as a process for issuing you with a security pass, any IT or PPE (personal protection equipment) you need.

Some organisations have either formal or informal guides where someone is your key point of contact for an initial period with responsibility for showing you round and how things work.

- **Occupational health** – in some workplaces, particularly those where there are any identified health risks you may need to have health tests. One of my businesses operates metal presses so ear defenders are compulsory on the shop floor and all staff have to have their hearing tested when they join and then again on a regular cycle.

- **Skills training** – there may be specific skills you need in order to be able to work (when I joined an accountancy firm after university the first two weeks were straight onto a residential course on double entry bookkeeping before I even saw the office), or there may be work specific processes and procedures that you need to learn (*Here's our Standard Operating Procedure for quality checking our widgets*).

  In either case, you will need to establish what training you are expected to have and how this is being organised.

- **Any choices you need to make** – your organisation may offer employees a range of benefits as part of their remuneration packages. The range of benefits on offer usually increases as you get more senior, but you may still need to make choices about whether to join a pension scheme, for example, so you need to be clear about this as such benefits will normally be trade-offs against salary.

- **Organisation chart** – it's very useful to get a copy of an organisation chart (or organigram) if you can. This is a diagram showing how the organisation is structured and who reports to whom. It will help you see how the part you are working in fits into the whole.

- **Expenses policy and process** – if you are going into a job which for example involves travel (such as sales) inevitably you are going to incur expenses for which you will want to be reimbursed. Organisations' policies will vary, and this is an area which can be very strictly policed, so make sure you understand what is and is not claimable, keep receipts to back up any claims, and know how to fill in and get your claims properly authorised.

Employers have to rely heavily on the honesty and discretion of their employees in respect of expenses, since by definition this type of expenditure often cannot be pre-approved. Employers are therefore very sensitive to any suspicions that their expenses system is being abused. So, filing any claim for dodgy or padded expenses is a very quick way to severely damage your reputation for honesty and get yourself into real trouble. Just don't do it.

- **IT equipment, access, training and support** – if you are taking a job which involves use of IT equipment then make sure you know who's responsible for sourcing this and setting you up, that you have all the passwords you need, training is arranged in any new or specialist software you are going to need to use, and crucially, who do you call for support when it stops working. Write that number down now somewhere you can find it easily.

- **IT policies** – on a related note ensure you are familiar with your organisation's policies on use of IT at work, both the organisation's and your personal devices. This isn't just about whether you can use your computer to surf the web at lunchtime but it will be about IT security. Being responsible for introducing a virus into your organisation's IT system because you've not complied with rules governing security, and plugged in that old memory stick of yours, or clicked on a dodgy website, could be a severely limiting career move.

   These threats are real. Whilst finishing this book one of my businesses suffered a ransom ware attack, which encrypted all our files, meaning we lost a whole week's transactions and had to do a full restore from our back-up.

- **Time recording** – many organisations will want you to record your time as this forms part of their process of assessing costs on projects or billing services to clients. If you don't want accounts breathing down your, and worse at this stage, your boss's neck, about missing timesheets, ensure you understand what you need to do when about recording and reporting your time.

Why have they employed you?

But before we get into more detail in the following chapters about how to manage your working life, it's not uncommon to develop some nagging doubts during those early weeks and months about whether you can cope, so here's a couple of things to think about by way of a bit of reassurance.

Remember, they hired you – that's important

You have been hired. The organisation which has employed you spent time, effort, and cold hard cash, often quite a lot of all three, in looking to find, interview, select and engage someone; and out of all the people who went into the find part of the process (and believe me, there's likely to have been a lot), they chose you.

So, always remember:

- they've not hired you for the fun of it, they've done so because they have work that needs doing (probably lots of it as you are possibly finding out)

- they have picked you to do it; and

- they (particularly the individuals involved in the recruiting process) are invested in you and you making a go of it.

After all, having spent all that time, effort and money, don't you think the people who were involved in hiring you are going to want the process to be seen to be successful? If it goes well they've got bragging rights about what a good choice they made in you haven't they? But if you don't do well, or even leave, then that's a pain for them; not only might they look bad in front of their colleagues for having got it wrong, but the likelihood is they are going to have to go through the process all over again.

The bottom line? Once you have been hired, whatever it feels like, people will be wanting to make the job work for you so they will be motivated to help and be supportive. All you have to do is manage this the right way.

But what if I don't know how to do the job?

If this is troubling you as a question it's worth asking yourself what they hired you for (and spoiler alert), it's not usually your skills or experience.

There are broadly three things that employers can be looking for in a potential employee and these are:

- **Skills** – your technical ability at the task.

- **Aptitude** – your natural ability for the task.

- **Attitude** – your behaviour towards the task.

A well-used recruitment mantra is *Hire for attitude, train for skills*.

This reflects a view that your attitude towards the work will be driven by your personality, which is something that will be really hard to change (for more on this see Chapter 3); whereas particular skills can be taught (and for some entry level positions there may be no assumptions about you having any previously acquired technical skills at all).

In some rare cases employers who want to train people in their own particular approach can deliberately look for people with little or no technical skills or prior experience in an area so that they can start with a clean sheet.

Whilst *Hire for attitude, train for skills* seems a sensible approach, it is however a little simplistic as training someone with aptitude is easier than training someone without.

I personally have the hand-eye coordination of a sack of cement with the athletic physique to match. However much I might want to, be keen to learn and be prepared to put the effort in, my aptitude for developing the skills required to become a world class ping pong player is therefore abysmal. If an organisation wanted to hire someone to train for this role, whatever my attitude, I should quite rightly come last on the list of possible candidates.

In taking you on your employer will have taken a view on your skills, or even lack of them, and will have decided to hire you taking these into account, usually because they felt your attitude and your aptitude were actually what they were looking for.

And if they are happy about your attitude and aptitude, given that they know what they were looking for in respect of your job, then really, who are you to argue?

3   Managing yourself

I was applying for a job as a senior manager in the restructuring team of one of the big professional services firms. Their recruitment process was something they evidently took very seriously, for obvious reasons, and the interview process was billed to take most of the day, with two face-to-face sessions and some psychometric testing.

The interviews seemed to have gone quite well, but then the Human Resources person appeared for the scheduled session to give me feedback on my tests, and she was obviously nervous. She sidled around the subject for a while as if she was unsure about how to broach what she wanted to say, and the longer she took to come out with it, the more I wondered what the issue was. Had I come out as an axe wielding psychopath? Or was there a real problem?

Eventually she got around to it. The problem was, she told me, my profile indicated very strongly that not only was I very confident in my decision-making ability, but that I was very prepared to back my decisions by taking action.

Now at this point I was struggling to see the problem. After all I was applying for a job in business restructuring, involving work to save businesses which are going bust and running out of time, where the need to take and then implement quick decisions was in my view one of the key aptitudes required.

But in her reading, this equated to a degree of recklessness in my approach which the firm could not possibly risk, and so suffice to say, there wasn't a meeting of minds and I didn't get the job, thank goodness.

You'll find as you go through this book that very little of it is about actual work, how to do this or that.

Instead most of it is about how to manage at work which comes down to understanding and managing yourself and then understanding and managing your relationships with others.

People are both individuals and types

You will already recognise that everybody you meet is different, with their own personality traits, act in certain ways, be interested in particular things, and be motivated by, and fear, different things.

But you'll also be able to generalise some of the traits you see in people around you into types. Know any introverts? Know any extroverts? How different are they in what they want and what they respond to?

A lot of work has been put into assessing various aspects of personality in the work environment, so as a very simplistic introductory example imagine a (highly caricatured) organisation with only two different types of people in it:

- **Square pegs** – The owner and founding entrepreneur is someone who is driven by success (and fears failure). He has recruited go-getting sales staff in his own image who tend to be competitive in outlook, seeking praise and (as public as possible) recognition and rewards while fearing rejection. Both the founder and the sales staff tend to shoot from the hip, being quick to take decisions, and are restless, active, and open for change.

- **Round pegs** – However when it comes to assembling widgets or processing the paperwork, to provide the customers with a reliable high-quality service, the firm has sensibly employed very different people in its operational administration and production functions. These staff like to have a structured, ordered environment as far as possible within which to work, with a clear understanding (preferably in writing) as to what the standard operating procedure is which they need to implement in order to deliver the right result to the specified quality standard, time after time. These staff tend to value security (so they know where they stand) and their relationship with their co-workers, while fearing change, and disliking uncertainty or conflict.

To make this type of organisation work you'll probably appreciate that:

- There is great potential for the two types of staff (and their respective functional departments) to get into conflict with each other (with sales complaining that production aren't flexible enough to deal with the customer requirements and delivery times they are landing; while production complain about sales lobbing half scribbled ill-defined customer requests over the wall with no consultation, no consideration of the current work schedule, and are then off to their next customer visit in their flashy company car leaving operations to try and sort out the mess);

- The two types of staff will need to be managed in very different ways to get the best out of them (with clear targets of sales to achieve and lots of praise for success for the square peg sales staff, and detailed instructions on how to do their particular job for the round peg production staff); and

- The business owner in particular will need to adjust his personal style to manage the round peg staff.

What sort of peg are you?

If you had got a job with this organisation and were naturally either a square or a round peg, you'll appreciate that whether or not you would enjoy it and be successful would be hugely influenced by whether you were joining the:

- **Sales department** – where if you are a square peg you'll fit in fine so long as you can cope and perform, but as a round peg you would hate the unstructured nature of the work and insecurity of the competitive environment; or

- **Operations department** – where if you're a round peg you'll find an environment that suits you and the way you like to work, but if you are a square peg you'll soon be chewing the walls with frustration and boredom at the rigidity of the processes and repetitive nature of the work.

To see how you best fit in to your workplace your starting point is that you need to understand yourself, which is where psychometric tests come in useful.

What types of psychometric tests are there and how should you treat the results?

In being interviewed for your job you may have had to take some psychometric tests already (if you have then it's usually considered best practise for the employer to give you some feedback on what your results were as in the case I've already described).

Some of these may simply have been designed to assess your aptitude and technical skills for the job in question. Applicants for a job involving coding for example, might be expected to take tests involving mathematical or logical reasoning skills.

But others will have been intended to find out more about your personality and working styles and it is this type we are interested in here.

Now I'd suggest that all these tests, and the interpretations of their results, need to come with some caveats:

- We're all complex individuals with unique sets of experiences, genetic inheritances, and personal emotional backstories, so while tests can give some very useful headlines and indicative characteristics, in my view no-one is truly categorisable and completely explainable as simply one of say 16 personality types.

- Most of us change both over time with experience and developing confidence so your personality changes and develops as well, and is not a fixed quality.

- In fact, we change from moment to moment depending on what's happening around us and our emotional state, with people ranging from being very steady and unemotional to those who are highly changeable. Whatever your underlying personality type, it may in practise vary significantly on a day to day or even minute to minute basis.

- We also change to suit circumstances (are you exactly the same person at home as you are at work?) so again our personality type may differ in different circumstances.

- Most of the tests are based on questions about what you would do if X happened or ask you to apply descriptive words to yourself, so the answers will depend quite heavily on your self-image, which may or may not be particularly accurate.

- Particularly when you are starting out on your career answering questions on how you imagine you would react to a particular situation can obviously be a bit speculative. Once you have been working for a while you may find answers based on your actual experiences are quite different.

- Importantly also, the feedback you get is likely to be from someone who has had a limited amount of training in the use and interpretation of the techniques with the simple intention of being able to operate them to the degree judged necessary by the employer to get the result the organisation needs. They will generally not be an expert with a deep understanding of the methodology, theory, nuances and limitations of the particular analysis being used and their feedback of the results will normally be based on a limited number of pre-scripted standard descriptions of what particular combinations of characteristics are likely to indicate.

So, as rules of thumb I'd suggest you:

- Do take the results seriously and take what value you can from them to help you understand yourself, how you work and manage yourself; but

- Take all results and the commentary or feedback you are given about them with a substantial grain of salt;

- Do not allow them to oversimplify your own analysis of yourself and other people; and

- Do try to take them again at points during your career to refresh your view, as you are likely to find your answers, and hence your profile, change over time.

I'd also suggest there are two types of psychometric tests that you should be aware of and, if possible take, covering:

- **Team working styles** – the Belbin Team Role Inventory.

- **Personality type** – typified by tests such as Myers-Briggs or Thomas Personal Profile Analysis (PPA).

Belbin Team Role Inventory (Belbin test)

The Belbin test came out of studies at a leading business school into how high performing teams work. It is used to assess how a person behaves in a team environment and their relative tendency to operate in each of nine possible team roles (where they will often naturally gravitate towards the same set of preferred roles in most situations).

It is widely used in business as findings have shown that balanced teams where all the roles are covered by the people in the team perform better than unbalanced ones.

It's important to you as one of the things you will quickly realise at work is that you will generally be working as part of a team rather than simply as an individual, so if you want to be successful, making a success of team working is vital.

The nine roles are:

1   **Plant** – creative ideas generators. Teams need these to come up with innovative solutions but too many in a team and you will be overwhelmed with off the wall ideas. Also, just because the team has then decided on which idea to pursue doesn't stop the plant from continuing to come up with new ones, which can be distracting.

2   **Resource Investigator** – the team's link to the outside world and the one who tends to kicks things off by sourcing what's needed to start with through their network, even if they then don't necessarily follow through right to the end.

3   **Co-ordinator aka Chairman** – usually ends up organising and managing the team, making sure everyone's involved and understands what's been decided and what's needed, but also delegating all the work so they end up with few, if any, actual actions themselves.

4   **Shaper** – shakers and movers, they are all about getting things done and driving for delivery. Get behind them or get the hell out of the way.

5   **Monitor Evaluator** – are the very necessary check and balance on the team with the ability to step back and take a clear view. Being analytical and prepared to take their time they are right much more often than they're wrong so are always worth listening to, even if you don't like what they have to say; but going too far they can end up being over critical and become a negative and demotivating influence.

6   **Team Worker** – are the treasures who keep everyone working together, diplomatically managing conflicts and stresses in the team. Often unappreciated or seen as weak and indecisive (that's you I'm talking to Shapers), due to their natural focus on maintaining good working relationships, you'll miss them if

they're not there as your team spends its time bickering rather than delivering.

7   **Implementer aka Company Worker** – know someone who insists on turning everything into a set of SMART objectives (see Chapter 4), is serious about their loyalty to the company and will take on the jobs everyone else hates because they need to be done? You've met an Implementer whose personal motto is probably *Make a rule, keep a rule*. Just don't ask them to be spontaneous or bend a policy.

8   **Completer/Finisher** – is dedicated to ensuring everything is exactly right when it goes out the door. And right to their own high standards, not just to whatever anyone else thinks is good enough. So, depending on your point of view they either go the extra mile to ensure perfection, or are nit picking perfectionists who can't delegate to save their lives.

9   **Specialist** – are technical experts, tending to focus on, and enthuse passionately about, a very narrow field, with limited ability to contribute outside of this aspect.

When I take this test my cluster of preferences in order are:

1 Shaper

2 Plant

3 Resource Investigator

4 = Chairman and Team Worker

Looking at myself and how I behave in meetings I recognise that regardless of my official role in any such group, I do tend to act in one or more of these roles depending on:

- what I feel the meeting requires to drive it forwards; and

- how, and how well, I feel other people are filling roles (eg if there's a Shaper who's driving the meeting well in the way I think it needs to go, I won't try and challenge or take over just because I have that as one of my preferred roles; but if feel there is a weak Chairman, then I'm afraid I do tend to just take control of a flipchart and pen to structure and manage the process).

Understanding your set of preferred team roles, and an awareness of what others might be, can help you fit into a team more swiftly and can support you in making it as productive as possible.

Myers-Briggs

Myers-Briggs (and related 16-type approaches) is based on the psychological theories of Carl Jung and one of the most used personality tests in business with some people wearing their INTJ (or whatever) as a badge of pride.

The approach looks at your preferences (and note this isn't about skill or ability) as to how you go about gathering and using information for decision-making across four scales. When thinking about the paired alternatives it's important not to be judgmental, despite what might be your own strong preferences, that one is in any way better or more valid than another, not least because the usages of some of the terms are very specific and need to be distinguished from their everyday meanings:

- **E = Extraversion vs I = Introversion** – is not used in quite the popular sense (note the spelling difference from extroversion) as this scale is about tendency towards action and interaction with people. Extraverts crave action and are energised by it and while they take short breaks for reflection before getting back to acting, inactivity over any longer period of time drains them. Introverts by contrast are more thoughtful, wanting to reflect long and hard before acting and engaging with people and then go back to reflecting.

- **S = Sensing vs N = INtuition** – are concerned with the way you deal with assimilating and processing new information (**Perceiving function**). Sensing is a preference for tangible (in quite a literal sense) specific data that can be referenced and checked. Those with this preference are looking to know the detail and hard evidence. Intuition is a preference for looking for the patterns that underlie the data to be able to construct theories and understand the organising principles which lead to the observable data.

- **T = Thinking vs F = Feeling** – is about your decision-making processes (**Judging function**) and again the usage in this context isn't quite what the popular understanding of the words might lead you to expect. They are both about the rational processes you apply to the data you have discovered through Sensing or Intuition. It's simply that thinking in this context involves a tendency towards a somewhat detached or analytical approach based on strictly applying causality and logical rules to arrive at the right result and finding dealing with illogical, emotional or erratic reactions very difficult (think Spock). Feeling by contrast tends to involve a much more emotionally aware and nuanced decision-making process taking into account the situation, people's feelings and needs to arrive at the best result.

- **J = Judging vs P = Perceiving** – is about what aspects of your personality types you tend to show to the world.

    Judging people will highlight their judging **T/F** score. So, a profile with **TJ** will come across as highly logical and probably task focused, while an **FJ** profile will be much more emotionally intelligent (or aware) and probably more people focused.

    Perception people will favour their perceiving function **S/N** score. A profile with **SP** will present a focus on practicalities and hard facts, while **NP** profiles will be seen as having a tendency to abstract thought and theorising.

How you score across these four scales gives a matrix of 16 personality types and you will find a variety of descriptions and interpretations of each group of characteristics online.

I retook a form of the test while writing this chapter and came out as INFP, a type characterised as The Mediator (there's a profile online at www.16personalities.com/infp-personality, which I found interesting, referencing as it does a strong urge to write).

Obviously, the idea is that by taking the test and learning your own set of characteristics, this can help you understand yourself and how you will be seen by, and interact with, those around you.

Thomas Personal Profile Analysis

A widely used commercial test, this is based on a short questionnaire where you are asked to think of yourself at work and ascribe a choice of descriptive words as most or least like you.

The results of this test are transcribed to give you a score across four characteristics to give you your DISC profile:

- **D = Dominance** – a high D score indicates a tendency to be motivated by a desire for power or control and a fear of failure, high Ds are focused on achieving results and can be directive, even autocratic individuals who will tend to Tell.

- **I = Influence** – a high I score is someone who thrives on recognition and praise while fearing rejection. They tend to work with and through people in a way that can range from a Sell to outright manipulation.

- **S = Steadiness** – a high S score indicates a desire for security and acceptance as a team member. Well suited to service and support functions they like procedure, working with people and will listen.

- **C = Compliance** –people with a high C score are often found in areas requiring technical expertise; they love facts, figures, a rule book to operate by and their motto is *Write it down*.

These are scored on a range of high (being what you like) to low (being what drives you) where the greater the distance towards the extremes of the possible score, the more intense the factor (while at the real extremes there is also a risk recognised that individuals can flip over into the opposite characteristic under certain circumstances).

Your scores are ranked in order:

- highest in intensity order; then

- lowest in intensity order

to give a profile summarised as say DSIC or CSID.

One of my issues with the psychometric tests discussed already is that they provide a single snapshot result and this is a point on which PPA scores significantly in my view. Not only does the PPA approach recognise the risk that people's reactions can swing widely at the extremes as discussed above, but the results are always mapped onto three graphs:

- **Work mask** – how you operate at work under normal circumstances;

- **Under pressure** – what your behaviour changes to when you are under pressure; and

- **Self-image** – how you see yourself.

In giving this range of related views, PPA goes some way to dealing with some of the caveats I outlined earlier.

Excuse me but I'm an introvert

I started writing the first draft of this section by saying if you are an introvert (like me) then there's good news and bad news, but of course the first thing to say is that the world is not simply this binary. While some people will clearly sit at either end of the scale, for the most part extroversion/introversion is a spectrum and people can exhibit ranges of behaviour in either direction.

Having said that, the good news if you do tend towards introversion is you're not alone. It used to be thought that about 25%–30% of the population are introverts, although it turns out many of us may have just been too shy to say so, as current research suggests the figure is more like 50%. So, while you sit there alone, actually, you're not.

The bad news is that traditional corporate cultures generally seem to have been set up to reward extrovert behaviours which are seen as leadership skills leading to promotion, and hence a self-reinforcing cycle. Think about where you are working and ask: Does everyone get a say or does the loudest voice prevail at meetings in your organisation? Does self-promotion or self-effacement move you forward? Is constant communication seen to be the way to be noticed?

This is also reflected in everything from the way people manage (extrovert managers tend towards expecting to tell people what to do, while introvert managers tend towards expecting their staff to think for themselves); through to how workplaces are organised such as open plan offices (how on earth is anyone supposed to concentrate in one of these?) which are fine for extroverts who are energised by constant interaction with people, but problematic for introverts who need to be able to have time on their own to operate effectively. Although as someone who would happily squirrel myself away and not talk to anyone all day I realise that to a degree natural introverts do need to be encouraged to engage with the rest of the staff (occasionally at least).

As someone who is sitting here writing this book on my own in my home office room, and by a strange coincidence has fled life in cubicle land and is now self-employed (and broadly unemployable), what advice can I give you on how to manage in an extrovert world?

Well one piece of good news is that the value of introverts and their skills are increasingly being realised. (See for example Susan Cain's book *Quiet: The Power of Introverts in a World That Can't Stop Talking*, or Jim Collins' book *Good to Great* which points out that some of the most effective senior managers are those who are self-effacing and who put others and their organisations above themselves and their egos, particularly it seems amongst some of the tech sector.) As a result, some organisations are trying to develop practises which are more introvert friendly so as to reap the benefits of the more considered approach introverts can bring to an issue.

However, there's no getting away from the fact that unless you are sitting at home typing a book, work is normally going to involve interacting with other people and so you are going to need to find ways to adapt and cope with this social environment.

- Use new technologies to communicate at a distance rather than face-to-face if you find it easier.

- Seek to work in smaller groups and meetings rather than larger if this makes you feel more comfortable.

- Acknowledge your introverted tendencies and the team role preferences which tend to go with this as you can then offer to play to your strengths as part of a team.

In addition, given that you are likely to be somewhere on a spectrum rather than at a fixed binary point, you can look to explicitly move out of your comfort zone and develop and use extrovert behaviours by setting yourself targets to say speak up at the next team meeting and make X numbers of contributions (and there's much more on managing communications in Chapters 7 and 8). By succeeding with small steps, you can become steadily more confident and able in using this set of behaviours whenever they are useful to you.

Assertiveness skills

But before we go too much further, some questions for you:

- Are you someone who has trouble stating your opinions (particularly when you think others may disagree) or saying No?

- Do you find it hard to ask for what you want, and do you often feel taken advantage of or just taken for granted?

- Do you feel anxious or resentful of the things people expect from you, or the way you are treated?

- Do you feel your contributions are ignored? Do you find your ideas being put forward by other people who then get the credit?

- Are you held back by feeling that you don't have a right to ask for things or to be considered, or fear of the social consequences if you do?

- Do you feel you automatically have to do something, just because someone has asked you? Is Yes your default option?

- Do you go along with things so as not to appear rude or awkward, or avoid giving your opinion as a way of avoiding conflict? Do you feel disagreeing with people is impolite and just leads to conflict and bad feelings?

- Do you have a passive communication style where you wait for others to speak or give their views first so you know what's safe to say?

- Or do you overcompensate, and aggressively try to dominate the conversation?

I'm hoping you've not got too much of a high score, but if many of these are feeling familiar then you probably need to work on your assertiveness skills, something we will come back to a number of times in this book (and you will need to read Chapter 6 on Managing To Say No).

So what is assertiveness (and almost as important for your perception of it, what isn't it)?

At it's simplest, being assertive is about:

- being honest to yourself and others, about how you feel and what your needs and wants are

- being prepared to communicate these to others (otherwise how are they expected to know and take them into account?)
- allowing yourself to accept you have as much right to your views and needs, and to be taken into account as anyone else (and expecting this to be recognised)
- while taking responsibility for, and ownership of, them; and
- respecting the rights of others to have their own requirements, as well as the information and opinions they can provide
- which you in turn will take into account.

As such, it's the basis for having an open and honest relationship with people where everyone's needs are respected and communications of these feelings and wants are made in a non-judgmental and unthreatening way.

One of the main barriers to you acting assertively will be your perceptions of what this means and how others will perceive it, so you may believe assertiveness is:

- just about selfishly pursuing your own ends
- all about always getting your own way
- rude and inconsiderate of others as it's always about me and about asking for what I want.

But just because you are honestly stating how you feel, this isn't forcing people to go along with you. Remember the point above that this is about mutual respect. You respect other people's opinions, wants and needs and their right to express them, don't you? So why shouldn't you have the same rights and expect them to do the same?

After all, people are always going to have differing opinions on any subject, so why shouldn't yours be treated with the same respect as anyone else's?

The good news about assertiveness skills are they are just that, a set of skills you can learn. They are not about who you are, they are about how you behave.

The bad news is that if you lack them, learning can be a difficult process as it means breaking some of the social habits of a lifetime.

These are what you will probably have used to manage all your relationships up to now, so changing can feel very frightening and risky as you take your first steps.

However the benefits of achieving these skills can be enormous, life changing even, and not just in the ways you might think.

Yes, they can obviously help you get more control of your life and what happens, building your confidence, self assurance and self esteem. But equally importantly, they can also help you interact better with others, allowing you to operate in a genuine way to build up more honest and open relationships.

Elsewhere in this book we will talk about a simple three step formulation of What I like, What I don't like, and What I want, but here, as we're focusing on assertiveness, is a five step outline describing script which expands on this and which you can try using as an alternative whenever you want to ask for something:

1. **Describe the other person's situation** – *I know you're probably busy*. This demonstrates you are thinking about them.

2. **Describe the issue as you see it** – *I know this job is urgent but I'm not sure I understand exactly what needs to be done and I know I'll need some input from you*. Be factual and non-judgmental.

3. **Describe how you feel about it** – *I'm feeling stressed as I'm worried I won't be able to deliver this job on time or properly for you*. It's very important that here you talk about your feelings, and avoid turning these into judgments which can be challenged.

4. **Describe briefly and specifically what you would like to see happen** – *I'd like to book half an hour of your time after lunch to go through the file and brief me on the issues*. Make this as positive and collaborative as possible.

5. **Describe what the positive outcomes of this are going to be** – *I can deliver just what you need for when it's needed which would make me feel a whole lot better*. Ideally these positive results should benefit both them and you.

If you find starting a conversation difficult, another tip is to preface what you want to say by in effect asking permission to say it.

Examples of this approach are:

- Do you mind if I suggest something?

- Could I just make a comment?

On the face of it these may seem extremely unassertive expressions as they are asking permission for you to speak. However, they are actually quite powerful tools for asserting that you have a point of view and that you wish to express it, as not least they are very difficult opening gambits for most people (other than the completely driven or actively rude) to say no to.

Similarly, if you find others taking credit for your ideas a simple formula I've seen used is to say: *It's great X supports my idea/agrees with me, but we need to get on and implement it by doing Y* (which should be a very specific action).

As I've said, assertiveness is a set of skills which you can learn (and there are courses and books which could help you) but which probably involve challenging some long ingrained habits. As with developing any new skills you will need to develop them through practise.

Even if you do decide you want to take a course, you shouldn't wait for this but should start today, as the sooner you begin, the sooner you'll see some results.

A good first step is to become an active observer of assertiveness in action and find role models to emulate. Think about people you know or those you see around you at work:

- Who seems to be assertive?

- What do they do? How do they act in ways which make them assertive?

- How do people react to them as a result? (And are they seen as rude and overbearing or are they actually quite popular? If so, why is that?)

- How and why does what they do, work for them?

- What techniques could you copy?

Bearing what you've learnt in mind, then:

- Rerun some past interactions where you feel you've been

unassertive and think about what you could have done differently. Try role playing this in front of a mirror, write out the lines you felt you could have said and practise them out loud. You can't roll back time to change that exchange but you want to get yourself into the frame of mind of being able to handle the next one differently.

- This is about learning and building your techniques so you need achievable wins to build your confidence. Plan for some specific interactions you have coming up. You will have meetings or conversations you know are coming, so pick some, preferably those you are going to feel most comfortable in and prepare. Think about what you would want to say to be more assertive and practise what you want to say and how you want to say it in advance.

- Put your plan into effect, and then review how it went. Ask yourself:

  o What worked, what didn't?

  o How did people react?

  o What would you do differently or try next time?

  If you can, seek some independent feedback from friends as to how you came across.

- Take your lessons and repeat, and repeat, and repeat until they become natural to you.

Celebrate your wins and never allow yourself to be overcritical of how you do. Remember you are trying to change the habits of a lifetime and that's going to be a long and sometimes hard road.

It's also the case that some people around you will have been very happy with your lack of assertion as it will have given them an opportunity to dump, bully or freeload on you (sometimes for years). As you start to be more assertive, be prepared for some kickback from these types of relationships as your changed approach and willingness to be put upon is inevitably going to make life less easy for them, and equally inevitably, they aren't going to like it.

But frankly, these are the sorts of relationships which are probably giving you the most grief and causing you the most anxiety and resentment, so the better able you are to deal with them, the happier you are going to be in the long term; even if in the short and medium term addressing the patterns of behaviour and expectations which have built up can be quite painful.

Have a balanced approach to your work and life

As we get to the end of this chapter, it's important also to remember that as a person, you are more than just the hours you spend at work, and that work shouldn't be all you do.

From time to time your working life will become stressful and may even make some unreasonable demands on you and your time which you may have to accept for a while. But as you start out on your career you should try and cultivate the habit from the outset of maintaining a reasonable work life balance.

Given modern working practises, this will be particularly important if you are expected to, or later come to, work from home as the ease of distinction between time at and not at work will become very difficult to discern.

- Ensure you schedule real down time when you properly switch off from work, with no checking your phone or emails.

- Take exercise to keep yourself fit and to help take your mind off work.

- Actively work on cultivating your personal relationships and interests outside work, something we'll come back to again later.

Some final thoughts about you and others

Hopefully having read through this chapter and perhaps taking some of the tests mentioned will have helped you to understand yourself, your motives, preferred working and communication styles and roles.

It will have told you more about you and how you can best manage yourself, and crucially, how you would want to be managed by others, which is the first step towards managing your working arrangements successfully.

If you are a 'square peg' then at the very least realising this will help you in trying to structure your working arrangements with your boss in a way that helps get the best results for you and them. (*I like to work to a written instruction so I can make sure I've done everything right so can we compile a checklist for me to use?*) But ideally, as you move within the firm and opportunities present themselves you can then look to find where there's 'square peg' work available, organised in a square peg way, working for a boss who appreciates and values square peg people and manages them in a square peg way.

If you are a 'round peg', then that's the last department you are going to do well in so you'll be looking to shape your career and seek work in a more 'round peg' friendly environment.

So, understanding your motivations can help you manage you and your work.

But of course, you aren't the only person in the organisation.

Each and every one of your co-workers and bosses will have their own personality (yes really, even your boss's bosses up to and including the CEO actually has a personality, normally at least). They will all have their own motivational preferences, likes and dislikes, ideal team roles and natural ways of working (and as a result may be better or worse suited to, and more or less comfortable, in the jobs they hold).

When in later chapters we start to look at communicating with people, and managing your co-workers and bosses, remember the sorts of team role preferences people may display as well as the range of personality types that these sorts of tests can highlight. Look to see how these may apply to the people you have to deal with every day.

If you can understand them and their preferences better, then you can better give them what they want, in the way they want it – and doing that is one the key secrets of success in the workplace.

4 Managing your time and work

I once bought a business supplying into the automotive industry as a turnaround project. In common with all the other companies in that particular supply chain it was measured and ranked (very publicly as a list of monthly comparative scores was sent to all suppliers including our competitors) on two delivery performance metrics:

- **OTIF percentage – On Time In Full**, the percentage of times we delivered exactly what we said we would, when we would – vital for a customer running their factories on a Just In Time basis where they ordered parts for delivery to the production line just when they were needed; and

- **PPM** – the quality measure of the number of **Parts Per Million** that we delivered which were out of specification; whether it was delivered on time or not, we still needed to deliver parts that were right.

The bad news was that the week after we bought the plant, we were called to what was described as 'a main offenders meeting' with a customer's purchasing director to be told a) we were one of the worst performing suppliers on their list, and b) he wanted to know what were we going to do about it.

You are a supplier of services to your boss.

The likelihood is that your boss is not looking for you as a new starter to come in and immediately shine as a star, transforming the business from top to bottom.

Instead they are looking for you to be someone they can dependably rely on, in other words they will want to see that your work is delivered, on time, in full, and right.

So, what's their perception of your OTIF and PPM scores?

And crucially, how should you work so as to give them what they want?

The temptation is to simply think you have to constantly be working harder and harder to keep on top of what's being thrown at you. But that way lies burnout and stress.

Instead you need to understand how you might be able to work smarter.

Before carrying on with all the things you are trying to juggle at the moment and thinking about **what** you have to do next specifically, instead I'd like you to stop and think about **how** you need go about working generally.

In this chapter, we're going to work through organising you and how you work to make life easier, and you more productive which means organising:

- your workplace

- your time; and

- your approach to work.

Organising your workplace

Take a look at your desk or your workstation. How well organised is it to support you in what you need to do?

How your working space is organised will have a real impact on everything, from how efficiently you work and how easy it is to find (or lose) things, through to health and safety as well as how you feel about your work.

Good manufacturing practise is to organise any working environment using the principles of 5S which was one of the foundation stones enabling Just In Time production. The approach has wide applicability to any workplace. Including your desk.

If necessary come in over the weekend and make a start on working through the five steps of a 5S process which are:

1   **Sort** – the first stage is to clean up the area. Remove everything that you do not need for what you are currently doing. Yes, everything. Put it somewhere you can find it when you need it.

2   **Set** – the motto of this stage is *A place for everything and everything in its place*. Organise the things you use for work so that the items you need most are the easiest and quickest to get at, with a clearly defined home, while things you need only occasionally are put away. This not only creates more room where you need it but also reduces wasted time in finding and

fetching what you need most.

Depending on the nature of your work and the equipment you have to use, this step can also be an important help with maintaining health and safety in the workplace.

Then keep track of what you actually do use. Anything you've not fetched to use after three months you should be asking yourself if you really need it at all.

3   **Shine** – means then regularly cleaning and tidying up, and inspecting your workspace as you go. Is everything you need available and ready for use? Does anything need repair or renewal? Or has anything crept onto your desk that needs to be put away again?

4   **Standardise** – is normally about ensuring conformity of approach across all aspects of the working environment by the creation and implementation of a structured approach and agreed sets of rules, so it's probably of less immediate relevance to you at this stage of your career.

An organisation implementing a full 5S process may, for example, look to ensure all workstations are identically configured to allow a particular task to be carried out. This way, any employee can use any position with exactly the same tools and resources at hand, and know exactly what the expectations are about how they should leave that station once they've completed their task.

5   **Sustain** – the hardest part of any 5S programme is, however, keeping it up and turning what is initially a one-off exercise into a habit through custom and practise.

To maintain the benefits of adopting a 5S approach to organising your working environment requires a disciplined focusing on keeping up those good working habits until they become second nature.

And keeping up your 5S organisation will take time in itself which you will have to set aside. Not only in setting it up in the first place and then instituting the regular shine process, reviewing your position and resetting your standards and taking any appropriate action.

While 5S as an approach seems a very simple thing, it is something that can have a huge impact on improving the:

- efficiency of your work, helping you to work smarter and avoid distractions and clutter

- quality of your work, helping you to avoid mistakes and errors; and

- safety of your work, by reducing the risk of accidents.

Organising your time – time management

Remember the measure, On Time In Full?

It's very easy to be busy in business. There are always things to do, deadlines to meet.

It's more difficult to be productive. There are always things to do, deadlines to meet and the tendency is often to do the quick and easy and put off the time consuming and difficult.

Are you just too busy sometimes? Do you have impossible deadlines? Do you never have the time to sort out your inbox?

A busy fool is someone who is rushing around, always under pressure and always doing all sorts of things, but crucially, never actually achieving anything of value, and unfortunately, it's a very easy habit to get into.

You need to avoid falling into this trap, and the key to doing so is how you prioritise and manage your work.

You often can't control what you are given, but you can control how you choose to deal with it, which in the first place means basic time management, which is simply about how you arrange and control how you spend your time.

The key steps involved in successful time management are:

- Understanding Urgency and Importance, and using these to prioritise your work.

- Managing and controlling your work through To Do lists.

- Mind mapping to structure your approach.

- Ensuring you have SMART objectives.

- Reviewing your workload and how you organise it; and

- Managing interruptions, because they are going to happen.

It's difficult to overemphasise the importance of good time management to the quality of your working life (and your life outside work as well).

- At a basic level, it will help you become more organised and by helping you feel more in control of what you are doing it can give you a clearer view of where you are going and more confidence that you are going to get there.

- Because it will involve you looking at what you are doing and why, it can help you to identify and cut out wasteful activities allowing you to achieve more with your time.

- By helping make you more productive (and helping you to avoid impossible deadlines and workloads) it can help you shine, enhancing your career prospects at work, and enabling you to do more of the things you want elsewhere.

- And by making your workload balanced and more manageable, it can make it less stressful and more rewarding.

As you progress in your career, if anything it will become more important as you take on more responsibilities, so it's good to develop good working practises as early in your career as possible.

Urgent and/or important?

You only have a set number of hours in any day, finding the time to fit everything into your busy schedule is often a problem, and there's nothing worse than feeling at the end of it that nothing has actually been done properly (or even at all).

But the aim of successful time management is that you are productive rather than just busy.

And often if you look at what you are doing, you will find you are busy without actually achieving anything, because you are spending time on things that don't really contribute to what you want to achieve, and not putting your time into the tasks that really matter.

The starting point is to therefore ensure you understand both the urgency, and the importance of each task on your list, and use these to prioritise your work.

Once you know the relative importance and urgency of each task, then following Stephen Covey's approach in The Seven Habits of Highly Effective People, you can rank them across what is a typical management 2 x 2 matrix:

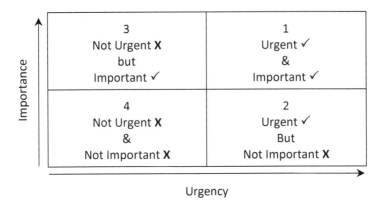

Once you have your tasks allocated across this matrix you can then choose how to deal with them:

- Focus clearly on those which are both **Urgent and Important** as these are the key tasks to deliver value in the short term.

- Then tackle the noise, the **Urgent but Not Important**, to get these out of the way (as if you don't do them you may ether miss a deadline, or at the very least they will be a source of interruptions and distractions until they are done).

- Then you can put the rest of your time into progressing the **Important but Not Urgent** which will deliver value in the longer term, where without the interruptions of the noise you can devote higher quality time (some people prefer to swap the priority of this and the Urgent but Not Important).

- As for the **Not Urgent and Not Important**, well you need to avoid spending any time on these other than to look at how you park them (as they may become urgent or important later) or preferably clear them off to someone else to do.

Sorting your work into these tiers is the first step to helping you achieve control of your work and avoid those feelings of panic and chaos that come from being busy all the time.

Instead you can now be as productive as possible within the time that you have as your effort is focused on doing quality work on Important items, while hitting the deadlines required for the Urgent.

Your To Do lists

Your daily To Do lists (you do have one, don't you?) are the cornerstone of organising yourself to get things done as they help you prioritise, plan and focus.

There are various formats (see further reading for the one I use) but whatever approach you decide on, the key points are:

- **Writing it down** – the simple act of committing your tasks to paper gets them out of your head and helps you to stop worrying about forgetting anything you need to do.

- **Prioritising** – you want to use your time as valuably as possible so use the Urgency/Importance matrix to group your work in order of priority (noting down any deadlines that need to be met so you can focus on these first).

  Sometimes however, whatever their actual urgency or priority, it's very useful to take the conscious decision to tackle any particularly unpleasant tasks or things you really want to avoid first. If they are things you are going to have to do eventually, all you gain by putting them off is to have them hanging over your head all day until you do actually do them.

  Whereas once they are done, you don't have to worry about them anymore and can get on with the rest of your day.

- **Structuring** – organise your To Do list into a way that works for you. You might, for example, group similar types of tasks such as telephone calls or emails you need to send so you can do these as a block.

- **Allocating** – put estimates of how long different tasks are going to take to see how they fill out your day and break tasks down into manageable parts that can be dealt with in the time you have available today, this week, this month and so on.

  By thinking about how long things are actually going to take, you can look to plan to give yourself enough time to do them and so avoid feeling rushed or pressurised.

When allocating time for a task, remember to include time at the end for checking it over and making sure you've got everything right before it goes off to your boss.

- **Rolling** – Your To Do list is normally about today, but in reality, it should be a rolling document, updated each day with projects and deadlines carried forward so as **not** to be forgotten. Again, see further reading for details of the format I use which includes a specific section on things to carry forwards.

One of the great things about To Do lists is how good they make you feel:

- Both before you start doing things, as now you have a sense of control, you are managing your workload which you've got corralled and organised down into a manageable list of things you are going to tackle in a known order, rather than the other way round; and

- As you do things, since ticking things off your list as you go gives you a real sense of satisfaction and achievement which can be very motivating in going on to address the next thing on it.

Mind maps

As a tip, if you are having difficulty organising your To Do list (or anything else for that matter), try mind mapping whatever you are looking to organise first to see if this helps you in structuring your thoughts.

You can create a mind map (or spider diagram) by hand and if you find it a useful technique there are software packages you may want to use. As a freer form approach than listing or tabulation of information it can easily incorporate a variety of interlinkages, and don't limit yourself to just words and a single colour if images and colour coding can help.

Drawing a mind map starts with putting your central idea or topic in the middle of the page, typically in a box or circle, from which you draw lines out to other topics, and then sub topics in greater and greater level of detail.

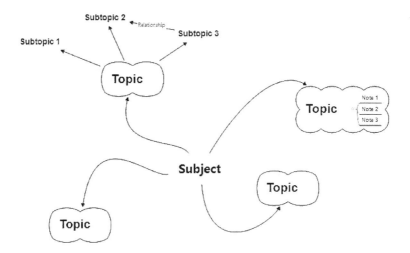

Mind map structure

As you post your topics and subtopics onto the map, you will naturally start to make associations between subjects which in turn tends to generate more ideas and help you analyse and assess whatever it is you are working on, as well as flagging up gaps that need to be filled.

As a graphical approach mind maps can hold and help organise huge amounts of information surprisingly effectively, whilst also being excellent tools for visualising and communicating ideas given their intuitive approach.

SMART objectives

SMART is a popular acronym in business used for setting objectives (although not everybody agrees on exactly what all the letters stand for).

The idea is that to be deliverable, or to hold the people involved to account for it, any project should be definable in terms of being:

- **Specific** – what is to be done – having a definition of the specific task, area or action involved. The goal involved needs to be unambiguous so everyone involved will know exactly what's expected as a result. Ask yourself: What you want to do and why.

- **Measurable** – how much is to be done – having a quantifiable way of assessing performance or achievement. The criteria for monitoring progress, keeping on track and motivating the team, and judging eventual success or failure need to be concrete. Ask yourself: How many, how much, how will I know when I've done enough?

- **Achievable** – can it be done – ensuring something is a realistic target. The goal needs to be set at a level which will stretch the team to ensure performance, but not be so far out of reach as to be demotivating as unobtainable and simply seen as providing a stick they will be beaten with. Ask: How realistic is the target level?

- **Relevant** – does it matter – focusing on things that make a difference, both to you, and those whose support you will need and who you will need to sell it to. Goals should be things that help drive you and your organisation forward. Ask: What will this achieve and does it seem worthwhile? Is it the best use of your time and resources right now?

- **Time bounded** – when is it to be done by – having a clearly specified timescale. Individual projects can tend to fall by the wayside, drowned out in managing the day to day, so having a clearly set (and realistic) deadline for completion can help prevent drift and create a sense of urgency to deliver on time to achieve the goal. Ask: When do we need this to happen, are we on track to complete on time and what should I do today?

Some versions for use with teams replace the A and R with alternatives:

- **Assignable** – who is to do it – having a clear understanding of who is responsible.

- **Realistic** – what can be done – having a realistic understanding of what is actually possible, particularly when taking into account the available resources.

If you haven't (or can't) broadly answer the above questions in respect of any project you are undertaking, you need to ask yourself what are you actually trying to achieve, how likely is it you'll succeed and how will you know when it's done.

When tasks are poorly defined or communicated enormous amounts of time can be wasted as the people working on them go off in wrong directions which contribute nothing towards progress, or go backwards and forwards with questions seeking the clarification and guidance which should have been given at the outset.

Without this sort of clarity any project is in danger of either:

- mission or scope creep, where no one is quite sure exactly what was specified to be delivered so it's never finished and becomes an open-ended drain on resources; or

- it's never finished and it just fades away as an incomplete waste of time.

Remember, being SMART is not just about setting goals, and the biggest tension tends to be between Achievable and Relevant.

Your SMART goals have to be things you can actually achieve so if a task is too big, (like eating an elephant) then it's right to break it down into manageable portions (like a bite at a time).

But it's equally important not to get bogged down in the detail, so always keep the bigger Relevant picture in mind so as to see how what you are doing fits in, and to keep on track to where you want to get.

Arranging to manage your workload

If SMART objectives can help you decide what you need to do, then working smarter is about how you go about doing it.

- **Record what you are doing – T**here's an old management saying: *What gets measured gets managed.*

  When you are looking at how to prioritise and plan your work going forwards, it's well worth keeping notes on a daily and weekly basis of what you do, when, and how long it takes, as it can show you a lot about how you might plan to do things better.

  Use a diary or day planner to keep a record of how you spend your time. Record what you do and how long it takes and take the time to review it on a regular basis.

  By using your work log you can look to see:

  o How long a run do you actually get at completing things?

  o What interrupts you, why and when?

o How much time was wasted, on what?

This last category can be the most difficult to work through, but the starting point as with many things in life is understanding your real position.

- **Organise your time** – Your computer will have a calendar system. Use it to plot your meetings, calls, time allocated to tasks.

And then regularly sync it across all your devices.

- **Focus on the important** – You will tend to make most progress on any task if you can give it your undivided attention. When you pick up a piece of work to do, try to make sure you stay focused on it and complete it before picking up the next one. Multi-tasking in a business environment usually simply means failing to do a lot of things, all at once, so just concentrate on actually doing one thing after another. That way things will actually get done.

Try to shape your working approach to allow you to focus on what you really need to do, and following the Pareto principle (or 80/20 rule) this means concentrating on the 20% of your work which delivers the key 80% of the value.

- **Have realistic deadlines** – Deadlines are extremely easy things to measure. There are only two options, either you meet them (On Time) or you don't.

Deadlines imposed by others will impact on your planning as essentially, they determine the urgency side of your prioritisation equation, while usually being largely out of your control.

You need to ensure you establish a reputation for doing things when you say you are going to, but this inevitably involves ensuring you give yourself realistic lead times, based on what's actually achievable in the real word as part of your SMART planning.

And this realistic approach needs to include an allowance for contingencies. You need to provide time in your planning for the fact you will be interrupted because that's just life (but as discussed below, while you sensibly need to allow time in your schedule for these you should still ty to manage them).

It sounds obvious, but to be On Time, you need to know what the required deadline is, so if you are not told when something is wanted by, make sure you always ask.

If you're not given a deadline by the person giving you the work, then decide on an appropriate one yourself and let them know when you are intending to deliver it by. This way they either have their expectations set, or hopefully will be galvanised into letting you know what the real deadline is.

An obvious problem arises therefore when you can see from your planning and scheduling a deadline you are given is unrealistic.

When this happens, your options are to:

o   Say nothing and fail to deliver.

o   Throw up your hands in horror and complain.

o   Proactively seek to find a way that the impossible can be achieved.

Needless to say, the more you can go to your boss with a plan or proposals on how the problem is to be managed and what's needed, the more popular you are going to be.

So how can you go about squaring this circle?

You need to explore different aspects of the problem to see whether any changes can help, so consider:

o   Firstly, how fixed or hard is the deadline? Can it be extended?

o   Could the allocation of more resources, the loan of an extra pair of hands say, be enough to get the job done in time?

o   Does everything need to be done by the specified deadline? Are there parts that can be left to later so that the key requirements are delivered on time?

If none of these are practical then you are going to need to make it clear, sooner rather than later, that while you will give whatever it is your best shot, you have to flag up that there is a severe risk that you will not meet the deadline.

The thing about not delivering on time is that people will notice when whatever it is isn't there, so while it's not great, telling them in advance is usually a whole lot better than having them find out by surprise on the day.

As a last resort, you can try asking your boss to help you with your prioritisation and agreeing your schedule; if something is going to be late then at least this gives them some choice as to what. But as I say, I'd use this technique very much as a last resort as other than perhaps in your very early days, your boss will be expecting you to be able to manage and prioritise your own work.

- **Be realistic about timing and what you can achieve** – When you are working, follow your priorities and your To Do list as much as you can without getting too distracted as new things pop up. A new task? Add it to your To Do list at an appropriate point.

Yes, you will need to be flexible to deal with things that crop up, that's why you need to build an element for contingencies into your planning, but as we've already discussed, the key to making progress is to focus on clearing your priorities, your must dos. After they're done you can turn to your lower priority items, your nice to get dones.

Set aside time to focus and just deal with what you are working on. If necessary let the people you work with know what you are going to do and how, and make it clear that you will only deal with urgent issues while you are concentrating on this. Then once you are done, put some time into catching up and clearing off the small stuff.

And be realistic with yourself. You really don't need to be in the office burning the midnight oil night after night. It's alright not to finish everything on your To Do list for the day.

There's always tomorrow, so always allow yourself some scheduled time at the end of the day to wrap up what you are working on and collect the list of things that you need to carry over into tomorrow as the start of tomorrow's To Do list.

Then when you do go home you can relax and switch off from work, knowing you've closed everything off as far as it can be, and you have everything you need to remember scheduled in for the next day.

- **Organise your paperwork** – Paperwork can be a time killer. Do you spend time going through piles of paper to find the thing you need to deal with? Do you spend time just sorting piles of paper?

  There is a very strong school of thought that you should only ever handle any piece of paper once, the idea being, you pick it up, deal with it there and then, and dispose of it by filing as appropriate, even if it's in the round metal filing cabinet under your desk.

  For devotees of this approach you essentially only ever need at most two folders:

  - **In** – for papers you have received but have not yet touched (as you will want to regularly schedule time to work through these as a batch rather than allow the arrival of individual pieces of paper to interrupt your work on your priorities), and

  - **Filing** – for papers you have dealt with (if you want to do your filing as a batch activity).

  This is a very useful discipline to adopt as it minimises wasted time in handling papers multiple times and so I'd highly recommend it.

  At the same time, I would recognise that depending on the nature of the work you are doing there may in practise be a need for a third folder called Pending, but this needs to be used carefully if it is not to become a drain on your time. It should only be for papers where:

  - you are waiting for some input from someone else, such as the answer to a question so you can process it correctly; and

  - you have captured that you are waiting to hear from this person on your To Do list.

  It should not be used to just store papers you have looked at and decided you'll get round to dealing with later as the likelihood is you won't. Instead, you will simply keep looking at them and keep putting them back into your pending file wasting time, time after time.

Deal with it and file it, or junk it.

- **Hold yourself accountable, and don't let things slip** – Look out for any other habits you have that are self-interruptions.

  Do you need the internet open for what you are doing? If not, why not close it? Do take regular breaks by all means, and do interact with your colleagues, but be honest with yourself. Is that trip to make a coffee really just an excuse to delay getting on with what you know you have to do? Is that chat while you make it really a time-wasting distraction from getting on with your job?

  You need to recognise what's helpful for you in doing your work and what's not adding value, and take action appropriately, which can be tough, but can make a real difference.

  At the same time keep an eye on what tasks seem never to actually get done. What are the things that never make it to the top of your To Do list?

  Why are they not being done? Are they things you are always putting off, either because you don't want to do them or because you are just focusing on things you enjoy, or on quick and easy things to tick off your list?

  And if these things are never getting done, what does that mean for you and your organisation?

  Are they things you need to try and pass over to someone else to do? Or are they things you need to bite the bullet and get on with tackling?

  If you do look to pass them over to someone else, do bear in mind that you may need to give them training in what needs doing which will take some of your time that you will need to set aside.

- **Give yourself time and the right space to work** – Try making a practise of getting up and getting into the office early, before the bulk of your colleagues are around. You'll be amazed by how productive this time is and how much you can actually get done before the day's interruptions start.

If you have something you need to be able to concentrate on during the day without interruptions, then see if you can find a suitable quiet working space where you won't be disturbed. Even in the worst open plan hells there are usually some break out or meeting rooms where you can grab some time to focus on a task.

If that fails, you could in extremis try a good set of ear defenders (and no I'm not joking, while you have them on they send out a real message that you're trying to concentrate which even the most gossipy co-worker can find difficult to interrupt). But only wear them when you really need to, as you do need to interact with your colleagues the rest of the time and be seen as a part of the team.

Which brings us on to...

Managing interruptions

It's all very well you setting out to be organised, but the reality of life is that interruptions and demands on your time will always come barging in.

So how do you manage to keep on track while this happens to you?

- **Meetings (bloody meetings)** – Unless they are properly run, meetings are often a huge waste of your time (and everybody else's). Managing your attendance at meetings and how they are run is an important part of your time management. Like anything else on your To Do list, you should be focused on being at those that are productive, for as long as needed (do you actually need to stay for the whole thing?), and avoiding everything else.

  There are whole books on how to run effective meetings so as a guide to starting out in work I'm not proposing to go into that. Here we are concentrating on you as an attendee of meetings.

  There are two basic types of meeting, regularly repeating meetings such as a daily stand up, a production planning meeting, or a regular project progress review; and ad hoc or project orientated meetings which are held as needed. And there are really only two basic purposes for having any meeting, which are to:

  o find (*How are we doing on this?*) and/or share (*Here's how we're doing on this*) information; or

o   make a decision (*We need to do this*) and assign actions (*We're agreed, the solution is that X will do Y by Z date*).

Anything else tends to just be a talking shop.

So, in respect of any meeting you are asked to go to, ask yourself what is the point of it? What specifically is it intended to achieve? Does anybody actually know? You would be amazed by how many meetings seem to be held apparently just for the sake of meeting.

Ensuring you are prepared is key to ensuring your meetings are productive. You are only going to get the right result if you have a clear idea of what you want to achieve once you are in the meeting. You can either wing it and try and succeed on the hoof, or you can do your homework and go in prepared. Your choice.

You should be able to tell what the meeting is for from the agenda, (which should be circulated in advance, otherwise how are you supposed to know what the meeting is about, what you are expected to bring to it, or how to prepare for it), and the attendees list.

If there are briefing papers attached, ensure you've read them (in my experience it will generally put you one up on most of the other people who are at the meeting).

If you or others are not properly prepared, then the likelihood is the meeting won't achieve what it needs to. And what will happen then?

Another meeting will be needed as a follow up to achieve what the first one was supposed to, which is a completely avoidable waste of time.

Remember the basics. Be on time, at the right place, and bring what you need to.

As a trainee in a big accountancy firm I once misread the time when I was supposed to attend an internal meeting, and as a result I arrived an hour early. As the speaker began it slowly dawned on me that a) the only other people in the room were all partners, b) what I was hearing was a confidential partner level briefing on the firm's strategy that I had no right to hear... and c) that my boss had just noticed me.

As a piece of advice on etiquette, at the top of this section I made the point that you might not really need to be there all the way through a meeting so it may be appropriate to try and avoid the irrelevant parts. However, this could be seen as disrespectful by the person who's organised the meeting, as you are in effect saying you have better things to do with your time than stay in their meeting. Take great care with any attempt to duck out of parts of a meeting. I would always suggest you approach the organiser in advance and ask them if they think you should stay on after the part which is relevant to you. This shows respect for their meeting, and gives them the choice as this way you are volunteering that you don't think you will be adding value to their meeting after a certain point.

And bear in mind as well that meetings are part of the social glue that binds organisations together; while a meeting you've been asked to might not be strictly relevant to your current priorities, it may be of value as an opportunity to learn more about the organisation and see and be seen by your colleagues.

- **Telephone calls** – Making telephone calls can waste your time as you wait on hold, have to call back time after time to try and catch someone, or play telephone tennis as you and the other person swap missed calls and voice mails; but at least you will have some choice about scheduling them. Answering telephone calls can both waste time and interrupt what you are doing.

When making a call always try and schedule it first with the person you need to speak to (or even ask them to call you if this is easier although this runs the risk of creating an interruption).

When you are working and need to concentrate on something, don't be afraid to put your phone on mute and use voicemail to take messages. Just ensure you keep an eye on it for any critical calls that you need to take, schedule time in your tasks to check your voice mail regularly, and respond in an appropriate timeframe.

If your phone diverts to others, make sure you brief them on what you are doing and how they should respond to calls. They will need to know when to take a message, when to put something through to you and how to answer the question: Do they know what time you will be free?

- **Your colleagues** – Your colleagues can also waste your time with interruptions, often without really meaning to.

  Sometimes it's a work-related thing, such as a task where they want your help and sometimes it will make sense to give it, and sometimes it won't, so if you don't want to waste your time you are going to need to say no.

  If saying no does not come naturally to you, refer to Chapter 6 for help on developing this skill.

  Other interruptions and wastes of time aren't work related but are more general socialising and gossip.

  Yes, you do need to engage with the people around you and become part of the team. But make sure you balance the amount of time you devote to this task with the other directly work-related ones in your daily schedule.

Your worst enemy? Your inbox

And crucially, don't interrupt yourself unnecessarily, which in the modern world means avoid letting your inbox run your life.

Your inbox will feel as though it is full of people shouting at you that they need things or a response now.

Some of these things will be important interruptions that yes, you do need to respond to, but by far the majority won't.

You have a choice, to run your work and your day:

- in a structured way you have planned; or
- by responding to the random requests, demands and priorities that other people fire at you through your inbox.

Which one do you think is going to be more stressful? Which one do you think is going to be more productive?

So, deal with your inbox in the same way you would deal with other interruptions. Avoid it so as to concentrate on doing what you actually need to do. Close your email if necessary and if that's not practical, certainly turn off instant notifications.

Then schedule specific times in your day to catch up, go through and deal with the noise of those emails as a specific exercise (remembering to properly file the emails in an appropriately structured set of folders).

A CEO I know who runs a consultancy and training business makes it known to all his staff and his clients that he does not read emails during the day, full stop. Instead he sits down at 10pm each night at his home office and deals will all the day's emails in a single session before he goes to bed. That way he can plan his whole day around delivery of what actually matters to his business and his clients.

Run your day your way, don't let your inbox run it for you.

Final tip for time management? Just say no

People at work and elsewhere are free to ask you to do all sorts of things which will take up your time, from doing a thing, to helping with a problem, to attending a meeting.

But just because someone asks, doesn't mean you have to do it.

It's your time, your life, your priorities, not theirs.

Sometimes you just need to give a polite no.

Is that an uncomfortable thought?

You can try reminding yourself that you need to manage your time. You can try considering that if they are free to ask, then it's only fair you should be equally free to say no.

But as I'd guess neither of these are necessarily going to help, coming up there's an entire chapter devoted to **Managing To Say No**.

Organising how you work

Remember the quality metric PPM?

I had a gap year job, it would be described as an intern role these days, where amongst other things I had to drive my boss around, well, his ban was only for a year.

And so, one time I dropped him, his wife and their two children at Heathrow airport to fly off on holiday.

I knew the date and time they were flying back and so there I was at the right time, sitting at Heathrow waiting for them to arrive.

The only problem was, I was in the wrong place, as they had flown back into Gatwick.

As my jetlagged boss, his wife and two tired children organised an unexpected and expensive taxi ride for them and all their luggage, just how reliable and dependable do you think he considered me?

The lesson I learnt? Never assume. Always make sure. And then check again.

You need to stay on top of your work and not let things slip through the cracks as that can destroy confidence in you and your reliability which can take huge amounts of time to rebuild.

So how do you organise your work to achieve the right quality standard every time?

Have systems, standard operating procedures, and checklists

The answer to that is to develop systems, standards and controls to ensure things are done right first time, every time.

In manufacturing circles, a Standard Operating Procedure or SOP is a written set of instructions specifying all the steps in any routine activity. The idea is that an SOP can give any worker the information they need to do the particular task properly which:

- promotes reliable quality through a consistent approach to the procedure and minimises variation in the way it is carried out and also minimises communication risks

- can be used to train new staff and as ways of capturing and spreading best practise (once you've invented it once, why waste time having other people have to invent if for themselves?)

- can improve efficiency as it's easy to find out how to do a new task

- can help ensure compliance with organisational, legal or regulatory standards; and

- support health and safety management (it's done this way to manage this risk).

SOPs should always be as simple, short and as easy to read as possible:

- giving a step by step guide, a flow chart is often ideal

- with clear and explicit instructions leaving no room for doubt as to what's needed.

As they capture the process and checks required, they are then often also used as the basis for checking or auditing work as the test is to see whether it matches the standard set.

And the same considerations apply to any tasks you have to perform on a repetitive or routine basis.

So, for example if you are involved in arranging meetings, you might have a checklist of things you need to remember to organise each time to ensure you cover all the details required to make it a success such as:

- **Who** – who is running the meeting, and who is expected to come. List the full names, contact and organisation details of all those who need to be at the meeting.

- **When** – the date and time, and if it involves any international contacts check what time zones they are in, and also any adjustment you need in notifications and invites to allow for British Summer Time.

- **How and where** – if it's a physical meeting check whether the booking has been confirmed. What are the address, contact numbers, directions, access, parking and refreshment arrangements? Is any equipment needed (flipcharts, projector, internet access?) and if so have they been organised?

  If it's a virtual meeting such as a conference call or using a meeting app you will need to know the call and log in details, as well as any codes required to join the meeting.

  Have all the relevant details been provided to all the attendees?

- **What** – covering both what is the meeting intended to achieve and what needs to go out and when to enable it to happen.

  What is the agenda? Are there action points or minutes from the last meeting? Do supporting papers need to be circulated?

To be prepared, attendees will require time to read any material so how far in advance do these need to go out? Does your organisation have a formal policy on this you need to comply with?

- **Will** – as in will people show up? Have the recipients confirmed receipt of the invitation and their attendance, does this need to be reconfirmed closer to the time? Can this be combined with a check to ensure they've received the papers they need?

- **Follow up** – the work on a meeting doesn't stop just because it's started. Who is taking down the minutes and the action points (otherwise why are you having the meeting?), who is responsible for circulating the output and is there a follow up meeting to be scheduled into the diary?

Hopefully you can see how the list of topics above could quite easily be transcribed into either a flow chart to set out the process of organising a meeting, or a checklist you could complete as you go to ensure everything has been organised.

You'll also hopefully see that had I a) had this sort of checklist and b) actually used it properly to check meeting my boss on his return from holiday, the result would have been me turning up at the right place.

This approach does however require a degree of self-discipline summarised in *Make a rule, keep a rule*, and a requirement to really use the checklist and actually consider and answer each question properly. If you continue to make assumptions that things on your checklist have been done rather than actually checking, sooner or later you will get tripped up.

Adding value and avoiding waste

Key to working well is ensuring the work you do adds value.

It sounds a simple thing, doesn't it? But have you stopped to ask yourself whether the things you are doing are actually valuable in that a customer would be prepared to pay for them?

Or are they wastes? In which case, you need to minimise or eliminate them as far as possible.

The classic test for waste activities, again much used in manufacturing circles is to look out for TIM WOOD(Y):

- **Transportation** – any unnecessarily moving of people, papers or products, as just moving something about does not of itself do anything to transform the product into something a customer is willing to pay for, so it is a cost incurred for no added value.

  In addition, every time something is moved or double handled, there is an additional risk it may be damaged, delayed or lost, so it brings a risk of higher costs.

- **Inventory** – refers to holding more material or products than are actually needed. Whether they are raw materials, work in progress, or finished goods, any inventory represents a cost that has been incurred without a corresponding revenue and carries a variety of further costs such as for storage, security and insurance. Any material that is not currently undergoing active processing to add value is a potential waste.

- **Motion** – whereas transportation is concerned with the costs of moving products and damage to the product, motion means the costs incurred on the production process through wear and tear over time, or say employees' repetitive stress injuries; or through specific incidents such as accidents which can injure workers or damage machinery.

- **Waiting** – is the time wasted whenever the material, information, people or equipment required is not ready. Whenever goods are not either being processed or being despatched to a customer they are waiting (and are therefore sitting as wasteful inventory).

- **Over-production** – is where you make more than your customers currently require. Manufacturers might want to run a large batch so as to avoid change over and set up costs, but this then leads to excess inventories and the risk of obsolescence if consumer demand or standards change.

- **Over-processing** – is where you process goods to beyond the standard the customer requires as they don't value and are not prepared to pay for extra knobs and frills they don't want or need. Any time or work spent on a piece beyond the customer's requirements, or work to a higher standard of precision, complexity or expense, is fundamentally a waste.

- **Defects** – is any work that isn't right first time. This is a very clear waste as whenever defects occur extra costs will be incurred in time and materials rescheduling the task and either reworking the defective item, or scrapping it and remaking the product involved from scratch; all of which are real costs with knock on effects in disruption and interruption to other work.

- **(Your people and resources)** – I have put this in brackets as it tends to be more an issue for managers than you in the early stages of your career, but for an organisation it is important to ensure all its resources, from its plant to the full potential of its people, are used. Just because someone has been employed to do X, if they have the capacity to do Y and/or Z then the organisation needs to recognise and take advantage of this otherwise it is wasting this potential.

So, when organising your work, always be watching out for TIM WOOD(Y) and try and eliminate him as ruthlessly as you can, as the time you save on him you have available for things your customers actually want and value.

And finally, a word about procrastination

Don't.

Deciding to do nothing about an issue, or to wait and see, are both completely valid decisions. So long as they are actively made choices based on an assessment of the pros and cons of a situation.

Procrastination on the other hand is a major time stealer as it turns small tasks into long term drains on your time as they come up and are put off time after time.

Reasons for procrastination can include:

- **Not knowing where to start** – is often a fear that the job is too big, or complicated, or difficult to understand. However, if you look at almost every big, complicated or difficult to understand job, you will see it is actually made up of smaller, simpler and easier to deal with component tasks, so start by picking one or more of these to complete. As you tick off each one, the rest will seem increasingly less daunting.

- **Not wanting to do it in the first place** – whether because it's unpleasant or just because there's something else you'd rather do. But if you don't do it you're not going to forget about it so it will be hanging over you as something you are going to have to face up to some time. Best to get it done and out of the way now, so you can fully concentrate on what you do want to do.

- **Thinking you can do it later** – which means that later you are going to have to think about doing this all over again, when you've already thought about it now. So why waste your thinking time twice when you could deal with it now?

Procrastination is a waste of time. And if there's a single lesson to be drawn from this chapter, it's don't waste your time.

5 Managing your co-workers and your boss, and working in a team

I'm involved in running a number of businesses so I end up going into a different office almost every day, often after having driven two or three hours to get there, and I have to admit I'm human (grumpy in the morning might be another word for it). I like to have a bit of routine when I arrive to help me feel I've got organised to face the day.

I like to get in, say Hi to whoever's around, pull my laptop out and plug it in, log onto the wifi to start downloading my emails, open my diary and To Do list workbook on the desk so I know what I've got on, make myself a cup of coffee, and settle in at my desk. Sounds a lot but really it's less than five minutes at the start of each day.

Then I'm feeling set up, organised, and ready to deal with the world.

So, how do you think I tend to react emotionally when I'm only just in through the door, I'm getting my laptop out of my bag and haven't even sat down yet, and someone comes rushing over with some complex detail problem that they want to brief me on and usually pass up the chain to me for a decision?

Inward groan? Irritation? Being honest, in all probability, yes.

Whereas if they'd waited five minutes until I was settled in and ready for business?

Well bringing me an issue isn't a problem, making decisions is generally what I'm there for.

My point is, the people you work alongside and for are human, and to make a success of working with them you need to understand what they want and need and how to manage your relationships with them. And sometimes it's the little things, like just giving your boss five minutes in the morning to settle down before you hit them with their first problem of the day...

This chapter is going to look at:

- Some general principles of how to deal with the people you are working with, including communication styles, and negotiation;

- Understanding your organisation's structure and culture, the context within which you are dealing with them;

- Teams and what's involved in working as a team; and

- Managing up or managing your manager, arguably one of the most crucial things you will need to do to make a success of your job.

General principles for making a success of working with people

If you want this in one line, it's **Find out what they want, and give it to them**.

Really, it's often that simple, however to put some flesh on these bones:

- **Get to know people** – to give them what they want, you have to know what it is first, so you need to build relationships.

  As you get to know someone try to learn about their plans, dreams and ambitions, everybody has them, as these will be what drives them, and determines what they want.

  And remember your personality type and team role preferences and how important these are to what you want and how you like to work.

  Well guess what, your co-workers and boss have personality types and preferences too, so think about what these are as you can use this insight to deliver not just what they want, but in the way they want it.

  And while I'm on the subject of other people and their foibles, always make sure you are seen to treat people with respect. Not just people above you in the organisation chart, but everywhere: up, down, and sideways. I don't care who they are or what they do, but everyone you meet is an individual with feelings, emotions and a value who deserves your respect, whatever they are doing and generally however they are acting; so giving it is just the right thing to do.

  Besides which, from a self-interest point of view, you never know who's going to end up where. There's an old saying about being careful about treating people right on the way up, as they can hurt you on the way down.

But a word of warning on relationship building. Be careful, as however friendly your work relationships are, your co-workers and especially your boss are not your friends (at least not yet).

You would expect your friends to be loyal to you. Would you expect the same of your boss? Your co-workers and boss are going to have other loyalties: to the organisation, their pay packet which puts food on the table, and their careers; which may well trump any friendship with you if there's an issue, so don't over share too early.

- **Deliver what they want** – which often translates into making them look good, so wherever possible look to set other people up for success.

- **Communicate** – this is the subject of a whole chapter but remember you are always interacting with people and your relationships will be based on how you communicate with them. Always be interested in them and how they are doing, ask what's happened and listen to what they have to say, whether it's good or bad.

  But when you do talk, remember to always be seen to recognise other people. If you're discussing a project talk about us or we, rather than I. Always recognise everyone in a team is a contribution to its success.

- **Be assertive** – just because you want to help others out, doesn't mean you have to be a doormat.

  To do what you want to do for others, you will need people to do things for you, so don't feel guilty about having someone do their job. Be clear and reasonable about what you need and when, so don't be afraid to ask for specific details of when something will be delivered, and then expect them to deliver on time in full. If that's the standard you are looking to deliver, why should you put up with anything less in turn?

And some Don'ts should go without saying, but I'll say them anyway. Don't be disruptive. Don't talk about pay. Don't gossip. And don't be a BMW, (Bitcher, Moaner, Whiner); if you've got a problem work out how to solve it and get it sorted.

Use communication styles appropriate to the person you want to communicate with

This is a subject we'll come back to in a later chapter but the key point to bear in mind when working with people is that we can differ in how we best express and take in information.

There are various different models of increasing complexity but for these purposes people are likely to have varying degrees of preferences for four main ways of finding out about something:

- **Visual** – some people like to take in information by seeing it. These are the real believers in a picture being worth a thousand words who respond to images and graphics as a way of representing information; use charts, graphs, symbols or diagrams to get your point across.

- **Auditory** – some people take information in by listening so you'll need to explain things to them, either through face-to-face discussion or by giving a lecture.

- **Written** – some people just like to take it in by reading and so you'll need to set out what you want to say in a document.

- **Kinaesthetic** – and others prefer to learn by doing, so if you can give them a hands-on experience or demonstration which allows them to experience the touch and feel of whatever it is, you will stand the best chance of communicating with them.

You in turn will have a style of communication which comes naturally to you. It probably sounds odd from someone who's writing a book, but I tend to think in pictures and if I'm communicating face-to-face I will be up at a whiteboard or flip chart and drawing diagrams and grids before you know it.

However, if you want to communicate effectively, then it's not just about you and what you prefer as a style. You have to get what you want across in a way that the other person can absorb and so one easy step you can take is to make your communication style appropriate to the person you are dealing with.

So, whoever you are dealing with, before you say, or draw or write or demonstrate anything, ask yourself, how do you think they, as an individual, prefer to receive information?

Negotiations

Many people's starting point in any negotiation is simply to ask themselves a variation on the old five finger question, **What's In It For Me?**

This tends to go with an assumption that negotiations are a zero-sum game in which for me to win, you have to lose. (*There's only enough cake left for one, if we both want it then one of us is going to go without.*)

But it's usually more productive to ask, **What's In It For Them?**

This is because life tends to be more complicated than a simple binary choice of winner and loser. In any negotiation people will tend to have a range of motivating factors, of differing levels of importance, and so it is often perfectly possible to obtain a win-win solution where each side gets the things they want the most, rather than an absolutist win-lose result (and in fact as we'll see there are a number of other combinations).

Which is why the **What's In It For Them?** question is such an important starting point for you. Because if you can structure your argument around that for what you want, how much more likely are you to get agreement?

Many of your interactions with the people around you will be negotiations of one form or another, it is everywhere around you at work and as with a number of topics I'm covering there are many, many specialist books devoted to it so I'm going to keep what I say quite limited to cover three points:

- What types of negotiations are there and why do they differ? Using Roy J Lewicki and Alexander Hiam's Negotiation Matrix from *Mastering Business Negotiation* to understand five different types of negotiation.

- What are negotiations about? Using the Onion model to distinguish needs, interests, and positions.

- What as a result, do you need to be clear about before you start any negotiation:

    o What are you looking to achieve and what are your alternative outcomes? As these will determine your objectives in negotiating; and

o What is your attitude and what do you think the other party's is? These will determine the type of negotiation.

Five types of negotiation

Do you approach every negotiation the same way?

The answer is probably not as both the relative importance of achieving the outcome and in maintaining your relationship with the other person will vary. As a result, Lewicki and Hiam developed their Negotiation Matrix showing when five different strategies are most applicable:

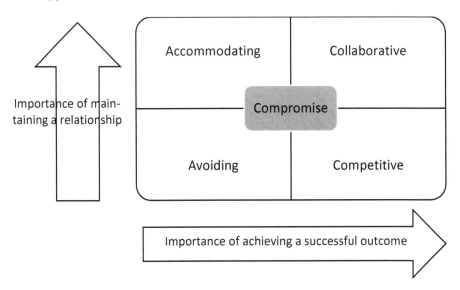

In this model the two driving factors are the importance to you of:

• achieving the outcome; and

• maintaining your relationship.

By assessing where you (and the other party) sit on this table you can work out which negotiation strategy is probably going to best suit you (and them). Then once you have started, if you observe which approach they have taken this can also give you clues as to how they see the position which can help you in assessing their priorities and adjusting your stance accordingly.

- **Avoiding (described as Postpone to Win)** – if neither the outcome, nor the relationship mean that much to you, why are you getting into a negotiation or conflict about it in the first place? You may therefore want to simply avoid the issue or negotiating on it altogether.

- **Accommodating (described as Lose to Win)** – if the subject of discussion and the specific outcome don't mean that much to you, but relatively speaking the person does, then how far are you willing to trade losing in terms of material outcome, for the win in terms of social capital or an advantage in a future negotiation. (*I let you have X last time, so now I think it's fair I have Y?*) Think about how explicitly you may want to make this trade as in order to appreciate what you are doing the other person needs to be aware of it.

- **Competing (described as Win-Lose)** – conversely, if the outcome really matters to you but you are not concerned about the relationship (think haggling in a market) then your negotiation style can be very competitive. Being successful with this style requires a clear understanding at the outset of what you are looking to achieve and what concessions you could make (as discussed below), and strong assertion skills to see your way through to achieving it. Questioning the other party as much as possible can help to get an understanding of their needs to help you with your bargaining; and funnily enough, despite it not being an objective, so long as you are fair and honest in your approach you can usually maintain a good respectful relationship with the other party.

- **Collaboration (described as Win-Win)** – if both the outcome and the relationship are important to you then you need to be looking to achieve a win-win solution where both parties achieve the goals which are most important to them (and this approach is also very useful if both sides face highly undesirable outcomes). Achieving successful collaboration requires a strong degree of trust between the parties, so open and honest communication of your goals are key, as are your reputation and your ability to come up with creative problem-solving solutions.

- **Compromise (described as Split the Difference)** – is the middle ground where you and the other party can't manage to fully collaborate but still want to both work together and each achieve some of your goals. When working towards a compromise you may want to use elements of the other negotiating styles in respect of specific issues and accept that you will have to make trade-offs, so it's vital you have a clear understanding of your goals and priorities.

In my books on buying and selling businesses I mention a rule of thumb: *The first one to mention price loses*, and this is a specific instance of a more general phenomenon which is whoever makes the first offer tends to be the one who comes off worst in any negotiation. Always wait for the other person to make the first move as it gives you clues as to how flexible they are prepared to be as well as what their priorities might be. Your compromises when it comes to counter offers should always be small to maximise your bargaining position, but focused as far as possible on addressing their key concerns so as to deliver maximum value to them.

What are negotiations about?

It may sound obvious but understanding what the other person really wants is usually critical to having a successful negotiation with them, but how often do you feel you really know this?

It can be difficult, as for a wide range of reasons people will often hide their real needs (either deliberately or even unconsciously), but this makes it very difficult to achieve a satisfactory solution which will endure in the long term as whatever is agreed now, isn't actually addressing their real needs.

The Onion (or Conflict Layer Model from *Working With Conflict* by Simon Fisher et al) distinguishes three layers:

- **Position** – how the person you are dealing with wants you to see them.

- **Interests** – the reasons they give to support their position.

- **Needs** – their real needs, which they may try to conceal as they feel they show them in a weak or even embarrassing position.

The idea behind this approach is by understanding the differences you can seek to focus on the needs which really matter to you, enabling you to communicate these openly to the other party.

However, this does rather presuppose you are engaging in a collaborative style of negotiation where both sides are looking to work towards a joint solution.

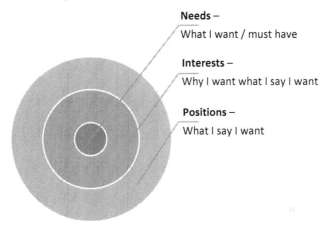

Needs –
What I want / must have

Interests –
Why I want what I say I want

Positions –
What I say I want

However, even in other situations where a collaborative style is not so appropriate, this is still a useful model for both:

- assessing your own real needs and priorities, and preparing your negotiating positions; and

- analysing and anticipating the other party's likely needs, interests and positions to help you prepare to deal with them.

To use this approach you need to work backwards from your position, or theirs if you are trying to anticipate the other party's needs, (*What you say you want*):

- **Define your position** – write down your position as clearly and precisely as possible, what you say you want to achieve.

- **Identify your interests** – working from this description (you may find a mind map or spider diagram works well for this) list all the reasons you would give to support these demands. If you get stuck, try keeping asking yourself the question, Why?

- **Identify your needs** – your interests are usually a means to an end so working further out from these on your mind map you need to look for what basic needs these interests are helping you to deal with (you may want to refer to Chapter 9 to help you understand more about understanding your needs and motivations).

You can normally tell when you've identified your real needs as you will recognise these are the things which you absolutely must achieve for you to feel the negotiation has succeeded; so they become your non-negotiable base line.

Use this understanding to negotiate to ensure you meet your real needs.

What you need to be clear about before you start any negotiation

From the above, to achieve a successful negotiation you therefore need to understand:

- What your and the other party's attitudes are to the importance of the outcome and the relationship, as this will help determine the appropriate style of negotiation.

- What your real needs are, as this will drive what you want to achieve from the negotiation.

However, in addition to these, you also want to think through your priorities, options and what you are looking to achieve, so before starting any negotiation you should always ask yourself (and seek to have answers to) three fundamental questions:

- **What's a real win for you?** – try to have a very specific goal in mind which you are looking to achieve. One of the reasons for this is so you have a point where you can stop negotiating, as it's not uncommon for people to have reached the point where they have essentially got agreement to what they want, only to then snatch defeat from the jaws of victory and lose it by continuing to negotiate.

    Once you have got to what you wanted, taking the risk of going for more or extending discussions should be an active decision as you may simply wind the other party up or give them the chance to change their mind. If you have the win you came for always consider banking it and walking away. Don't just get greedy and gamble away a real win.

- **What's your drop dead/walk away point?** – conversely, what's your bottom line and the points below which you will not go?

- **What's your (and the other party's) BATAN (Best Alternative to a Negotiated Agreement)?** – if you clearly understand everybody's alternatives then you are in the best position to make judgments about your respective negotiating positions.

Organisation structure and culture

But before you start looking at how you work with the people around you, it's useful to think about the context in which you are working.

Remember that organisation chart and employment manual you were given on your first day?

Do they tell you everything you need to know about how your organisation actually works?

No, they don't, because they are only half the story, if that.

Two of the strongest forces operating within and on an organisation, are its structure and its culture. It's important to understand what these are, how they are linked, and crucially, how they differ, as they will have a huge effect on how everyone around you works and behaves.

- **Structure** – is how the organisation is arranged and operates. As such it's something very formal that has been set in place by the organisation's management and is also very public in terms of things like job titles and those organisation charts, as well as being expressed in things like policies, processes, and procedures that are in the manual you've been given.

- **Culture** – is also how the organisation operates. However, it's about the shared values, experience and beliefs of the organisation. Whilst these days organisations will generally try to take steps to cultivate the culture the management aspires to, it is however something which is to a large degree independent of management, is informal and takes the form of war stories, in-jokes, reputations and myths.

  Because a culture grows up over time, is never formally set out, and forms such a pervasive background of *How we do things here*, this wood is often all but invisible to those working inside the business who only see trees. But despite the fact it's invisible and everybody in the organisation will have a slightly different interpretation of what it means, it's the crucial glue which binds the organisation together, defines who does (or doesn't) fit in, and sets all those unwritten rules which you are going to need to absorb if you're not to trip over them.

Structure determines if A is B's boss.

Culture determines what being boss is expected to mean here, from slave driver to supporter.

Different types of structure and culture

Each organisation will have its own distinctive culture derived from a mix of sources and influences including its history, its founders, its senior management, the way the firm sees itself, (Are we a sales focused organisation, or one focused on engineering excellence?) down to the type of employees it recruits, and where they come from.

While the details of each culture and structure will differ, there are some broad recognisable types and as businesses develop in size and complexity, the structure and cultural style often develop along parallel lines from:

- an entrepreneurial to a functional structure, and

- a power based to a role based culture.

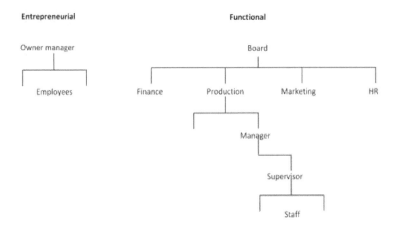

Structure types	Culture styles
Entrepreneurial: • an owner/manager who is in direct contact with all their staff	**Power based:** • an overall leader who makes or has authority over all the decisions
Functional: • there is a clear structure with defined hierarchy, levels of authority and lines of control	**Role based:** • job specifications exist and staff are expected to fulfil responsibilities and make decisions within a system of clear reporting lines, authority levels and a chain of command

There are two further common (if specialist) business culture/structure pairings which are:

Structure types	Culture styles
Matrix (see below): • teams are assembled involving staff from different functional areas to operate on a project basis as required, typically seen in consultancy firms or large engineering projects	**Task based:** • the focus is on forming teams to complete a specific task or project rather than performing a function or reporting lines within the hierarchy
Specialist: • individuals who band together to practise essentially as sole traders but with common support mechanisms. Sometimes seen in professional practices where barristers' chambers are perhaps the best example	**Resource based:** • as each individual is essentially practising on their own the individual's requirements will tend to take priority over those of the organisation

Matrix structures tend to evolve in specialist circumstances, for example a major engineering operation where each client project has a manager (A, B or C), whose job it is to manage the project on behalf of the customer by in effect purchasing services from the business's various departments such as production, HR, etc.

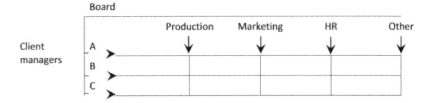

And of course, given that culture is ultimately created and driven by people and their views, an organisation's culture is not going to be consistent across all teams, departments, or locations. You may find the culture of the part you are in differs markedly from that in the office across the hall or the site down the road.

Understanding your organisation

A key step in working successfully within the structure and culture of an organisation is understanding it. Take the time to have a good look around to see what sort of place you've got yourself into.

To help you to understand what sort of an organisation you are working in, take a step back and think about its structure, culture and how they interact.

- **Structure:**

  o **Draw an organisational chart showing who formally reports to whom.** How clearly structured is it? How logically organised is it?

  o Take a different coloured pen, mark on your plan the **lines of power**, who goes to whom for decisions. Does this follow the formal structure? If not, why not? (For example, A is the factory manager, but all the lads on the shop floor still come to B as the boss for all the decisions.)

  o Put a **job title** by everyone on your chart. Do they make sense given the lines you have drawn?

  For each of the **key roles** in your business is someone shown as clearly responsible?

- **Culture:**

  o What words would you use to describe the way people work

together in your team/department/office. Cooperative or competitive? Challenging or supporting? Collegiate or hierarchical? Flexible or bureaucratic? Where do your choices start to change? Is there a point where it becomes us vs them?

- What do you think the organisation stands for? What does your team/department appear to think?
- What does it say its values are? Does it and its employees actually live them?
- How is conflict managed?
- Is everyone respected equally? If not, what attributes or achievements create respect in the organisation? Achieving sales? Getting things done? Professional skills or expertise? Looking after their team? Or delivering results?

Working in teams

One key difference you may find from school or university to work is the degree to which you will be expected to work as part of a team in many situations, either as part of your normal day to day activities, or on some ad hoc project. Some of these teams will be set up very formally with a strong degree of structure, set roles and strict project management, others will be quite informal groupings quickly arranged to get something done.

It's also the case that teams may not just be restricted to people within your own organisation, as it will be interacting with a wide range of other parties, from suppliers to customers, or business partners, or advisors. You may find yourself involved in teams involving not just people from other areas in your business (cross functional) but with people from very different businesses, organisations and cultures.

So, to make a success of working in teams, it's important you have an understanding of how teams work.

Creating effective teams

Forming an effective performing team is not just a matter of putting a set of people in a room and giving them a task, as to become a team the individuals have to go through a four-stage process usually characterised as:

- **Forming** – selecting the individuals to participate in the team.

- **Storming** – arguing about how the team is to work.

- **Norming** – agreeing how the team is going to work together; before then

- **Performing** – finally acting as a team to deliver what's required.

Any team will have to go through some form of this process in order to gel. For example, we have already covered that individuals will have preferred roles within a team and the members will have to find and settle into the roles that make sense both for them and the operation of this particular group.

Effective teams tend to share a number of characteristics, so when setting the teams' norms, it is beneficial to actively seek to develop these:

- **Appropriate shared values** – the team will need to work together so it will need to share an understanding and agreement as to how everyone in the team is to work together towards the common objective, and then deliver this in practise.

  This will generally involve a commitment to good, honest and open communication, recognising the differing contributions people will be able to make to the team, and a wish to ensure everyone's views are both heard and understood.

  It will involve a desire to both work as a team, with everyone taking responsibility for their own actions and helping each other so as to achieve the joint objective, and be regarded as a team with the output being recognised as a team effort.

  And it will involve some basic considerations of respect for each other and the team as a whole, such as a commitment to punctuality and regular attendance at progress meetings.

  In some cases, teams will adopt a formal code of conduct setting out a basic agreement as to how the team members commit to working together and treating each other.

- **Skills, roles and experience** – a group needs to have the right mix of people as resources to be able to succeed.

This means both people with sufficient ability in terms of knowledge but also an appropriate spread of Belbin team role profiles to ensure all the functions required to allow a team to operate effectively. If you want to deliver, do you have a Completer/Finisher? If you want to assess the options objectively do you have a Monitor/Evaluator?

- **A vision** – an overall goal the team is looking to achieve.

- **Clear goals** – whatever the overall vision, a group's goals should always be specified as tasks on a SMART basis so the objectives are clearly understood by all involved.

The steps to getting an effective team are relatively straightforward and involve:

- **Selecting the right team members** – This includes obvious things like the relevant individual's technical skills, knowledge and experience, but it also means having people who will work constructively with others, and who are willing to grow and develop within the team.

  Size of the team is also an issue with some thinkers suggesting that four people is the best size of a team as giving enough to cover off the team roles, whist being sufficiently few to be able to work closely together.

- **Having the right leadership** – there needs to be a team leader who is responsible for ensuring the team works together effectively, facilitating cooperation where required and making sure the team has the resources and information needed to achieve its objectives.

- **Setting its ground rules** – ensuring that all team members explicitly agree how the group will conduct itself helps to both reduce conflict, and increases productivity and effectiveness.

- **Defining its goals** – and as we've already covered, the team's goals need to be clearly defined in SMART terms as clear goals reduce any confusion as to what the team is there to achieve, and increases commitment towards an achievable end point.

But it's worth asking why you want a team to be effective. It may sound obvious but a well-functioning team has a wide range of advantages as:

- People tend to be more engaged, taking ownership of the problem and seeing how it fits into the big picture, and actively supporting the team effort.

- Effective teams have access to a wide range of resources in the skills, knowledge and effort team members will bring to the party giving the team a greater ability to solve problems and achieve results.

- For the team members themselves, effective teams give more scope for growth, development, and a sense of achievement, as well as just being more fun to be part of.

The care and management of bosses

When you are working you will have a boss, and in many ways this is going to be the most important relationship in determining how you get on in your first year at work. It's therefore worth giving some specific thought as to who they are and how to manage your interaction with them.

As with everyone else however, the same basic principle applies, to have a successful relationship you need to find out what they want and then give it to them.

Let's look at some of the main types of boss, think about how to understand them and their needs, and then set out some guidelines to dealing with them successfully.

What type of boss have you got?

Bosses come in a variety of flavours and there are many ways of slicing and dicing them into groups.

For me one of the most useful ways of thinking about the type of boss you have is to realise that someone giving you work can:

- set you high or low levels of challenge to perform (on all sorts of levels, and in all sorts of ways such as the difficulty or quantity of the work, the time pressure, or the standards required); and

- give you high or low levels of support by way of guidance, training, resources, or feedback in doing that work.

So, in best management tradition this gives a 2 x 2 matrix (and as a tip, if you every want a career in consultancy, there's very little in business that people don't try to get down to a 2 x 2 matrix):

Challenge	1 'To' Bullying	4 'With' Developing
	2 'Not' Absent	3 'For' Mollycoddling

Support

1 **High challenge/low support** – is a bullying, non-caring style where your boss does stuff To you. Typically, they will dump work on you in a demanding way, with little or no sign of appreciation for what's delivered, and often quite the reverse in terms of criticism of every failing. Not uncommon as a style in very old fashioned top down cultures, these bosses will just keep on driving you until you eventually die of overwork, at which point they get their next slave.

2 **Low challenge/low support** – is an absentee boss who basically ignores you. In this situation, you will receive no interesting or challenging work and you will eventually die of boredom and despair, forgotten and covered in dust.

3 **Low challenge/high support** – is a mollycoddling mother hen type who tends to do stuff For you whenever a question arises, so you have very little chance to try new things, stretch yourself, learn, or develop, and so you end up being kept dependent on others for ever which is not going to take you anywhere.

4 **High challenge/high support** – is someone who will work With you in a way that develops you and your skills. Make no mistake, they will be demanding, with very high standards and sometimes quite scary expectations that will make you feel stretched and which to be honest, sometimes you will fail to reach, because they are stretching. But they will also want to help you reach the standards they want to see you at, so they will be there to support you with advice, encouragement, understanding, time and resources (so long as they see that you are putting the effort

in on your side to working towards developing yourself which is what they want) – and any failures, so long as honestly reported, will be treated as learning opportunities.

Number 4 is the sort of boss you want to find and get to work for as much as possible since while it may be a tough gig, ultimately it's the most rewarding and developing way to go.

Understanding your boss

Your manager is someone who is:

- Busy, they will have their own responsibilities, and remember you've not been hired for the fun of it, you are there because they have work that needs doing and have made the case they need to spend money on you to do it.

  When they are dealing with you, you need to always bear in mind that they will have all sorts of other things going on in terms of tasks, projects and other people's interests to balance, and so much as they might want to, looking after you is never going to be the only item on their agenda.

- Unlikely to be completely independent and able to set all their own priorities and rules. In any organisation of any size your boss is going to have their own bosses to please, targets to meet and policies and procedures with which to comply.

- A human being, with a private life outside of work, and so in addition to their work considerations and pressures they will have a range of priorities, plans and issues they are also dealing with and which will affect their demeanour, none of which have anything whatsoever to do with you. Sometimes your boss has just got out of bed the wrong side in the morning and it is nothing personal.

- May or may not have had any training in managing people, and may or may not be a good manager (with or without training).

  There is often a tendency to promote people doing a job and to simply expect them to be able to manage others (their co-workers) doing it. However, this can be a difficult transition to make without support and for example typical strategies adopted by first time managers or team leaders asked to take responsibility for managing their workmates can be:

- o To try to stay everyone's friend as though nothing has changed, which is fine in terms of getting on with everybody but doesn't lead to respect or effectiveness in getting things done.

- o Become a tyrant and act as though the power has gone to their heads expecting that everyone should simply do what they tell them to do which can quickly breed resentment; or

- o Yo-yo between the two, trying to stay as everyone's friend until they get frustrated about getting things done at which point they snap into a rage and stomp around shouting and pulling rank until it all blows over and they try to get back to being mates again, the problem here being that none of the team ever really know where they stand with them.

What new managers need to learn is how to have a consistent relationship with the people they are responsible for managing, where everyone is clear about the standards required, and the support and commitment the manager will be giving back to their team.

It's not always an easy skill to learn as people will have differing aptitudes for management and as a result you may come across reference to the Peter Principle which suggests that people are promoted based on their ability to do their present job, until they get to a job which they can't do (their respective incompetence), at which point they become stuck.

- • Will have their natural operating style which can include:

    - o hard edged decisive task and results orientated, where people and feelings don't enter into the equation

    - o cold systematic and analytic data driven types, methodical in their decision-making; or

    - o warm team players, diligently getting on with the job and looking after their staff.

- • Will have their own approach to delegation (or not).

    Some are incurable micromanagers who are nervous about

letting go and want to ensure they have a handle on all the details, all the time, so they'll be peering over your shoulder constantly wanting to know what's going on and checking what you are doing.

Others take the view expressed to me by one boss of *If I've hired a dog there's no point in barking myself*, and want you to take over responsibility for getting on with your work, expecting to be called in as and when required on a management by exceptions basis.

Managing your manager

Your job is, in part, to manage upwards, to manage your boss and your relationship with them. So, the key things you need to do are:

- As we've covered in this chapter already, start by understanding what drives them, what they want, and how they like it. Then you can use this to decide what they need from you and how best to give it to them. Remember the points made above in that they are a person just like you, with bosses, targets, career, family life, aims and ambitions, so ask yourself what their goals are.

- Once you understand that, align your work with their goals and focus on making them and your team look good.

  Try to anticipate their needs:

  o Will they require information? Deliver it early.

  o What is their preferred communication style? Everything in writing and annotated to the nth degree and backed up by appendices of data, or summarised into a diagram on a single sheet of paper? Learn what your boss likes as an individual so you can give it to them in the way they appreciate and value.

  o Have they got piles of work to do? Take some of it off them. Stay late to get this extra stuff done (and don't go on about it afterwards – you are doing it because you want to help).

- Respect their time:

  o Be self-managing – you are there to help and support, not

be a drain. So be someone who organises themselves and gets on with their work managing their time to deliver On Time In Full at zero PPM without needing to be told to all the time. You really don't want *Works well when under constant supervision and backed into a corner* on your appraisal.

o Be self-sufficient – part of your job is to solve and deal with the various problems and challenges you will face. If something does come up, once you've got past your very early days, your first approach ought to be to try and figure it out yourself, rather than to go running to your boss all the time for instructions. Unless it's obviously really serious, only escalate something as an issue once you have explored the options for yourself, and when you do...

o Be self-starting – Margaret Thatcher famously commented that one of her ministers was a favourite because whilst everyone else came to her with questions and problems, he came to her with answers and solutions.

So, don't just raise an issue. This is called delegating upwards and is something that your boss is likely to find very irritating as a sign of someone who is not taking responsibility for their work and who is just pushing all the decisions on jobs back up to them.

If you see an issue:

▪ start by clearly defining what it is; then

▪ put some thought into establishing all the available options to deal with it (as well as the resources these will require)

▪ evaluate the advantages and disadvantages of each potential course of action, so you can rank them in order of attractiveness; before finally

▪ going to your boss with a plan (or choice of plans to authorise), preferably including a failsafe contingency plan by way of backup.

In short, bring them an answer to approve, not a problem to

solve.

- Be there for them and always deliver – become the problem solver, the go to person that everyone looks to when something needs doing absolutely reliably. Once you are indispensable, you will stay indispensable.

- Work on establishing a good, personable, professional relationship – the stronger the better.

   o   Be polite and friendly. They will have moods, they're human, don't let it get to you.

   o   Communicate, ensure they are kept informed about your availability. If you have time off coming up make sure they know about it and that appropriate cover and a hand over has been arranged, so they aren't left without back up.

   But crucially, don't overstep the mark. Even more than your co-workers, your manager is not your friend and both of you need to keep a professional distance. No matter how nice they may be, or how much you socialise, treat them with respect but don't share your innermost thoughts, or views on other members of staff.

- Finally, be loyal and supportive – good bosses will repay this and can become lifelong mentors who can help you with your long-term career (once you're not working for them). Poor bosses? Well not so much.

6 Managing to say no

I'm busy trying to make a living, sorting out problems and issues in the businesses I'm involved with, whilst also looking for the next opportunity and working on getting the next project off the ground.

So why do I currently have an unpaid job as a director of a professional body?

Because I said yes when I should have said no.

Why saying yes is a problem

Earlier in this book I've made a bit of a thing about your saying yes, particularly early on so as to show willing and establish the right first impression. And there's no doubt that in many ways it's good to say yes.

But in your working life you will be bombarded with requests and if you want to deliver On Time In Full with zero PPM, then the practical position is you can't say yes to them all.

Saying yes too often just ends up with you:

- mismanaging your priorities to deal with the latest request

- failing to deliver your core tasks reliably, and worse, getting a reputation for it

- spending your time doing things you don't actually want to do or worse, you don't enjoy

- losing your work life balance and feeling overwhelmed and stressed.

In short, the inability to say no is a ticket to underperformance and burn out.

Yes, you need to act as a team player and help out. Yes, you need to take on new things outside your comfort zone, but never forget you also have to manage your time and resources so as to be able to deliver what you've said you will, when you've said you will.

Taking on too much doesn't actually help anyone as it never ends up being done properly.

So, to manage your time and capacity all you need to know and use is one magic word.

No.

Why saying no is difficult

However, saying no can be very difficult and many people have real problems with it.

We are social animals and to help maintain our social bonds we often want to please others, so saying yes not only feels the easy answer, it is the easy answer.

So why is no so difficult?

It can be for a variety of reasons, which mostly come down to concerns about relationships and your self-image:

- on the positive side, you may be concerned to manage your working relationship with someone you expect to have to deal with again; or

- you may be concerned with building a relationship in the first place and generating positive impressions about your helpfulness and willingness to pitch in; or alternatively

- you may simply be concerned that the other person's feelings could be hurt and you don't want to risk that; or

- you are concerned about what people might think.

While all of these reasons for not saying no can have some validity in terms of how you need to manage your dealings with the people around you and your own emotions, they need to be balanced against your need to respect and manage your own time and commitments.

Why saying no allows you to say yes properly

When someone asks you to do something, you have the right to say no, whether it's to:

- **save your money** (No you really don't want to lend your mate money again since they've not paid back the last thing they borrowed);

- **save your sanity** (No you don't want to lend your car to your mate whose nickname is Crasher) or more usually in a work context;

- **save your time.**

Hopefully if you've read this far you'll appreciate you need to manage your time to:

- **deliver your priorities** (and shock horror they aren't always the ones where people are shouting loudest); and

- **do the things you choose to do.**

And picking up from above, sometimes it feels easy to say yes because what's being asked doesn't sound like much, particularly if it's a way off in the future when you're sure you'll be able to fit it in somehow. But it's surprising how quickly small things multiply and add up to big interruptions; and how quickly sometime in the future becomes now while you're doing other things.

Saying yes is easy and feels good, right up until you run out of time and fail to do what you've said you would; at which point everybody, but especially you, is likely to be wishing you'd said no in the first place.

Whereas if you say no to all the little time eaters and time wasters, what does that do for you and your time?

It frees it up to say yes to the things you really want to do, and have the time to actually do them.

So, stop worrying what people will think about you if you say no, and start thinking about what people will think about you when you can say yes properly (because you've used no to defend your time to be able to do so).

Should you say no?

One of the key reasons you need to learn to say no is down to managing your time and priorities.

But before you even get to this as a consideration, there are a number of practical questions you should consider about the sense of taking on the job as this basic saying no decision tree shows:

Does this need doing?	No?	Say No

Yes?

Are you the best person to do it?	No?	Say No

Yes?

Can you deliver? Do you have the time and access to what you need to be able to do it?	No?	Say No

Yes?

Is it worthwhile doing? Is it a productive use of your time compared to your other priorities that you will have to put off/delay?	No?	Say No

Yes?

Say Yes

A few of the most obvious ways of dealing with requests that you really should be saying no to will flow from this decision tree, as if you're not the best person to do the job then you can be signposting the asker to the person who is.

If you actually couldn't deliver for identifiable specific reasons then you can point to these as reasons why however much you might like to say yes, you can't take on the task as you know you won't be able to deliver and you don't want to let the asker down.

Not all nos will feel the same

Different people can ask you to do things, in work and outside, for differing reasons, with differing degrees of reasonableness. How you will feel about the request, and saying no if that's what you want, need or decide that's your answer, will depend on the circumstances and a range of factors:

- **Who is asking?** – Are they a close friend, your boss, or a complete stranger? Your emotional response and relationship considerations are going to differ markedly depending on who's asking.

- **What are they asking for?** – Do they want you to give them your time, your money, your advice, a kidney, or something else?

- **Why and how much do they want it?** – Have they told you? How important an issue is the request to them? And how much do want to let that weigh in your decision?

- **What does it mean to you?** – If they're asking you to support a cause you believe in as well you may be inclined to say yes. If it's for something you disapprove of then you're more likely to say no.

- **What impact does it have on you?** – How much of your resources is this going to take up. If I'm asked to give change to a charity collector in the street I might do so. If they ask me to donate all my savings, (if I had any) I'd probably say no.

- **Have they the right to ask you?** – Different people have the right to ask you different things in different situations. It's not unreasonable for your boss to ask you to do work related things, but there will be a point affecting your personal life beyond which their rights to make requests should not go.

  Socially too, someone who does things you ask them to might have some right to expect you will be inclined to reciprocate. Whereas you may decide that someone who never returns favours has run out of the goodwill to expect them.

- **Why are they asking you?** – How personal is the approach? Have they asked you specifically as the right person to help with the problem, or are they asking everybody? Are you just being asked because you're the line of least resistance, someone who they think will always say yes?

Overall you need to decide how you feel about it which often comes down to how reasonable you think the request is, rather than simply do I want to?

As covered elsewhere in this chapter, thinking through your views and responses in advance can help you in:

- **making your decisions** when the time comes; and in

- **being comfortable with the decision you've made** as you will know your no has come from a reasoned and thought through process.

The general principles of saying no properly

There are some basic rules which will help you to not only say no, but to say no effectively:

- **Put a clear value on your own time and priorities** – if you don't, why should anyone else?

  Whenever someone asks for your time you need to have a clear view of what your current commitments and priorities are, otherwise how can you judge where this request ranks in relation to them?

  But once you have made a judgment, then you have your reasoned justification for deciding to say no.

- **Prepare and crucially, practise your no in advance** – I'll come back to this below in more detail but it makes sense to think through how you are going to say no in advance and even have some stock scripts you can use.

  And once you have your scripts you are going to need to be able to use them, so you need to rehearse them so you feel familiar with and as comfortable as possible when you come to deploying them in real life.

- **Avoid the question before it's asked** – if you can forestall a request so it's never made then you don't actually need to say no to it at all.

  If your schedule is fully booked for the next two weeks, why not let the people who come to you with requests know you don't have any capacity in this period, and that you are focused on completing the tasks you have in hand?

  Some will take the hint and not ask (although once you are freed up it's probably politic to a) let them know and b) thank them for giving you the space to get done what you needed.

  As for those who don't and who still come to you? Well at least you can deal with their requests from the standpoint that they have done so in the full knowledge you have told them you are already booked up, so what answer should they reasonably be expecting?

- **Buy yourself time** – the easiest initial response can be as simple as asking if you can get back to them on it (perhaps once you've checked your diary, or got clearance from someone else, if you need to give an explanation).

  This does then actually allow you to properly consider how it fits in with your capacity and priorities and give a considered answer, rather than being bounced into a response on the hoof.

  If having done so you decide you can't help, then at least you can respond knowing you have given it proper consideration.

  It also gives you the opportunity to...

- **Use the communication style that suits you** – avoid face-to-face to start with if that helps.

  We each have different communication preferences and persuasion skills. Some are good at face-to-face communication, developing and delivering arguments on the hoof, some are much better by way of writing where they can structure the logic of their response and craft the language.

  So, when you need to say no, look to choose the approach that works best for you and if that's by email, then don't be afraid to look to use this as much as possible, particularly if you are still just looking to get comfortable with saying no.

- **Be prepared to keep on saying it** – again we'll come back to this below but some people won't simply take no for an answer and will pester you to change your mind.

  Be warned, once they find this works, none of your nos to them will ever be final. Just ask any four-year-old about the value of pester power.

  While you should always be prepared to change your answer when and if the facts or your understanding based on rational discussion changes (and not emotional blackmail), you do need to get the reputation for sticking to your decisions, so no means no.

- **No, or not now?** – while your no means no, this may often just be because of your current workload rather than a blanket decision for all time.

It can be appropriate to let the asker know that you might be able to help later, particularly if you can clarify that by giving them a specific timescale (*Sorry I can't help now but I'm probably going to have some time next week*), as otherwise you are opening a door for the request to be repeated incessantly. (*Hi, are you free to help now? No, how about now?*)

- **If you're going to say no, say it quickly** – when I ran a finance brokerage raising business loans we had a saying that a fast no was the second-best answer from a lender, as it meant our clients at least knew where they stood and weren't kept hanging on.

  Sometimes people try to put off saying no in the hope the request will somehow go away and they won't have to say anything that damages a relationship.

  Most of the time it doesn't go away and your relationship is damaged as the asker becomes irritated waiting for an answer.

  If it does go away however, your relationship is still damaged because the asker definitely knows that you've ignored them up to and past the point it was too late.

- **(Usually) give a brief explanation** – you may feel you need to give a reason to justify your no, as just a bland response can seem a bit harsh and discourteous, as if the other party isn't worth the nicety of an account.

  It is generally a polite move but when you do give your reasons these should be brief and they should be couched as an explanation of your reasons as you see them, not a plea for understanding.

  The reason for including usually in brackets is there are some people who will see the reasons you give as either:

  o excuses, giving them the opportunity to try emotional blackmail by arguing the relative merits of your reasons against the greater claim their request should allegedly have on your time; or

  o as issues, they can bargain or attempt to overcome so as to free you up to comply with their request.

Again, we'll touch on dealing with this below but you really do not want to get into debating the merits of your reasons. Remember, in the absence of a significant change in the facts or your understanding, your no means no.

- **Be polite, but not over apologetic** – carrying on from the point above, being courteous doesn't hurt you. But remember, they chose to ask you, so you have the right to choose to say no, so why should you have to apologise for managing your time?

  The danger is that an apology carries an implication that you have something to apologise for and it can make you sound weak or even open you up to emotional blackmail.

- **Be assertive** – the overriding lesson here is don't be afraid to respect and express your own needs.

  After all, if it's easy to grab your time just by asking for it, why wouldn't people do it? Whereas if you are robust in defending your time, eventually the time wasters will learn not to bother you as there'll always be an easier mark somewhere else.

  In many ways managing to saying no effectively can be a variation on a classic assertiveness formulation of structuring a response:

  - **What I like is X** – say something positive, in this case such as, *It's great you've asked me.*

  - **What I don't like is Y** – where you state your position or feelings about the issue, such as, *But unfortunately, I've already booked up to be at X all next week so I'm not here to do that for you.*

  - **What I want is Z** – where you state your requirements, which in this case is, *I'm sorry but I have to say no/I can't help.*

- **Offer something else to help** – of course just because you need to say no to what you've been asked to do, doesn't mean you don't want to be helpful, so always try to think if there's anything you can offer that would be useful.

  Depending on the request, this could be a wide range of things from links to information, to tools, or practical hints and tips.

If you are offering something else, do make sure it's something you can actually provide, obviously without taking more of your time than actually providing the help requested in the first place.

- **Divert to someone better placed to help** – an alternative to something else you can do is someone else who might be able to do something better. Do you have a contact or a resource that you can forward them on to?

  After all they've approached you but what the asker usually wants is help solving their problem, so if you can send them on (possibly with a personal introduction) to someone in a better position to do so, how helpful is that?

A generic no for all seasons

Following on from this, it's worthwhile having a basic outline structure you can turn to whenever you have to say no, which could be as simple as this:

- **Greeting** – don't forget to use their name.

- **Personal note** – optional, but in relation building terms it's always worthwhile including something personal and positive in correspondence (from something specific about them or their family, or their news, to the generic such as, *It's been ages since we've spoken*) whenever you can as a reinforcement that you have a personal relationship over and above this particular transaction.

- **Your thanks for being asked** – show why you are grateful they have thought of and asked you and be very positive about what they are doing (What I like is...).

- **What the issues are** – this is your chance to explain how this impacts on you or what the problems are which would prevent you delivering (What I don't like is...).

- **Your no** – don't forget you do need to clearly state that this is the decision you have reached: *As a result, I'm afraid I need to say no* (What I want is...) which can reference the issues above.

- **An offer of other support if you can** – wherever possible you should always try to offer something by way of a contribution if you can, whether it's something else you can do yourself, or by way of pointing them to other resources or people who may be able to help them with what they need.

- **A positive sign off** – just because you can't help this time you want to retain the relationship, so it's worth making the effort to do so. Even if you can't help you can hope their project goes well and is a success, can't you? You can also try repeating your thanks for being thought of, or ask to be kept up to date with their progress to show your interest.

You may then want to apply this structure to come up with a set of standard scripts to dealing with a variety of specific situations or requests you have to deal with on a regular basis.

Start out with some stock nos

Saying no gets easier with practise so to start with you might want to develop some stock phrases to deal with common specific situations.

Think of a few general problems you have had in saying no to requests, whether it's because you didn't have the time, resources, or the experience to deliver what was required, and use the template above to construct and write down the responses you should have given.

However, none of these are going to be any use to you unless you use them.

Now read each one out loud. How does it sound to you? How do you feel saying it?

Work on them until what you are saying fits your personal style and the culture of where you are working, continuing to say them out loud as you do so. Rehearsing them in this way may feel odd at first but if your natural habit is to always say yes you are going to need to retrain yourself to be able to say no, and the first step in this is to have some things you have managed to become comfortable saying.

You will probably need to be very deliberate in using these to begin with as an alternative to your normal reaction, but as you use them in practise they will soon feel a far more natural part of your range of responses.

Pick some easy nos to practise on

Saying no on the hoof to a request that's put to you can be the most difficult thing to get to grips with as it's very much a moving target where the initiative is with the requestor who can wait and choose their moment to pounce.

To practise your saying no skills to begin with, try starting with some sitting ducks.

There will be responsibilities or tasks in your To Do list you have said yes to in the past which you now wish you had avoided. Make a list of those you want to remove, prepare your script for the first particular issue, make sure you are comfortable with it, and then execute it to remove the problem from your in tray. Then repeat until you have winnowed your To Do list as far as you want to.

Apart from the time and heartache this will undoubtedly save you in the long run, the advantage of this approach is that it allows you to take the initiative in saying no and to practise it at your own pace to develop your confidence and familiarity with the techniques which work for you.

Problems in saying no – people who won't take no for an answer

It's all very well you saying no, but is that the end of it as far as the other person is concerned?

Sometimes it is and they will accept what you've said. But sometimes it isn't, so how do you deal with:

- **Not accepting no means no** – Sales people need to be persistent in search of closing a deal and so they will often be trained to assume that no always just means not now, and this mantra has then spread more widely into the world of work. Other people either just don't seem to respect your decisions, or are natural nags.

  For whatever reason, despite you having clearly and firmly said no, some people will simply continue to ask (distinguish this from any sensible process of debate on what the right answer should be or presenting relevant new information that you should realistically consider in your decision-making process).

  This can make you feel guilty but really, what have you got to be guilty about? It's your life, it's your decision what you say yes or no to, however desperate they may be.

In fact, it's actually quite a disrespectful thing to do to you as it's essentially saying your no isn't an answer that's respected, and they think you can just be nagged or browbeaten into acquiescence. So, bear that in mind as you may have to take assertive steps to deal with it using our old formulation:

o **What I like is** – *It's great that you've asked me to do X* (see, I really did understand what you want).

o **What I don't like is** – *But I've already told you that I can't or won't do X* (possibly because of Y if you need to include an explanation or context, but not an excuse, see below) and I'm not going to change my mind.

o **What I want is** – *So please stop asking.*

- **Seeking to work around or undermine your no** – It's often tempting, as covered above in formulating a generic no, to include some kind of explanation for your decision to show it's not just a casual rejection (*I'm sorry but I'm stuck doing this filing*). It often feels the best thing to do as a way of managing the relationship, but it can also signal some guilt that you've said no.

The risk here is that if you give a very specific reason as an excuse for not complying, some people can then seek to help you overcome this issue so that you can now say yes. (*You're too busy with that filing? Oh, that's OK, come and do this for me now and I'll help you sort those papers afterwards.*)

If your reason given was the only reason for saying no and this is a realistic solution that allows you to say yes, then that's probably fine and possibly even a win all round.

But if you wanted to say no for other reasons than this, then relying on an excuse hasn't worked.

So, if you really don't want to do something, don't just rely on a specific excuse. If you need to provide an explanation it needs to be a wider contextual one (*I'm sorry but I just don't have the time*) which is less open to specific problem solving by the asker.

- **Emotional blackmail** – is often used by controlling people where they trade on feelings of fear, obligation or guilt (collectively known as FOG) to achieve what they want in a relationship.

  Emotional blackmail can take the form of explicit threats to you by way of punishment (*Do X or I'll do Y to you*), explicit threats to themselves (*Do X or I'll do Y to myself*), or martyrdom (*Do X, I don't mind Y will happen to me*).

  For more information on understanding and dealing with emotional blackmail see Susan Forward and Donna Frazier's book *Emotional Blackmail*.

- **Can you really say no to your boss?** – if saying no is difficult because of social conditioning to want to please, then saying no to your boss, who you definitely want to please, and show you can handle your work reliably, is obviously particularly difficult. You may also be asking yourself, since they are your boss, why would or should they accept no?

  However, if that's what you are thinking, then you've already answered your own question.

  Your boss wants you to deliver reliably (**On Time, In Full**), with no mistakes (**zero PPM**).

  If your no is clearly and sensibly because you need to defend your capacity in order to deliver what they need in respect of your existing commitments, then why should your boss have a problem with this so long as it is properly presented and demonstrable to them in these terms?

Don't just get into a habit of saying no for its own sake

But finally, a word of warning.

Hopefully you will find that the ability to say no effectively, assertively and without guilt is empowering, but it's important not to abuse that power.

You need to remain positive in your approach to requests in life and at work and to remember, the purpose of saying no is so you:

- can do what you say you are going to; and

- are able to say yes to what you want to do.

It's not simply to be able to avoid agreeing to anything you don't want to do. Sometimes you need to take on things you'd rather avoid, and sometimes you are going to want to say yes to build social capital and bonds of reciprocity by taking your fair turn or being seen to be willing to help out.

Sometimes it's just as important to pay it forwards, or into the favour bank, as it is to manage your time now. After all, you never know when it's going to be your turn to be the one asking for help.

7   Managing communication

Emails are great. One of my businesses was in discussion with a prospective customer about what we might be able to sell them, when they sent us an email listing not only all the products and quantities they bought from our main competitor, but also the prices they were paying. As you can imagine it made pitching our prices and our sales negotiations a whole lot easier.

But why on earth did they send it to us you might ask? Why give away such a key aspect of their bargaining position? The prices we had to beat?

Well of course they didn't, deliberately that is.

It was just that someone their end had forwarded on an email in answer to a particular query about a specification, without checking the full trail that came with it. Whereas when we read back through the history about half a dozen exchanges earlier we hit pay dirt.

Why communication is important

Communication is one of the key tasks you'll be doing at work.

Want something to happen? You need to communicate.

Want to let people know what you are doing or have done? Communication.

Whether it's face-to-face, or in writing by way of reports, presentations or email, you will spend most of your time interacting with and communicating with other people, so it's a key skill to get right.

Do it well and you'll shine.

Do it badly, and the best you can hope is that no one ever finds out.

And the starting point for successfully managing your communication is simply to remember that not only are you communicating all of the time, but that you need to do so purposefully and effectively.

The BBC's mission as set out by Lord Reith and against which its output needs to be judged is to Inform, Educate and Entertain. So, what's the point of your communication? Next time you are going to speak to someone, or write them an email, stop and ask yourself:

- Why am I doing this? What am I trying to achieve?

  Do I just want to inform them, *Hey project X is complete* (and if so why)?

  Am I looking to convince them, *Hey, we did a really good job on project X, finished early and under budget, so the team deserves a reward*?

  Am I talking about the past, *This is what happened*? Or about the future, *This is what we should do*?

  Am I trying to argue a particular point of view? Or do I need to give a balanced and impartial overview?

- Who am I communicating with? My boss, a co-worker, a client? What formality of tone and style might each expect?

- Are they insiders or outsiders? Will they be experienced in the technicalities of what I am talking about (where excess explanation is superfluous or even counterproductive), or lay readers (who will need to be introduced to basic terminology to be able to understand what I am saying)?

- What is the best way of communicating so as to achieve the result I want? Is this something where a face-to-face chat might work, or does it require a formal report?

Communication takes many forms and while there are some general principles which apply across all types, for the purpose of this chapter we're going to divide the subject into two main groups, being:

- **Face-to-face –** most obviously verbal communication where one of the most important things to realise is that it is by nature a two-way process and so communication is not just about you speaking. Instead it's about you interacting with the other person and so your ability to listen is equally, some might even say more important.

  Equally vital in face-to-face communication but often overlooked is the importance of non-verbal elements such as body language and eye contact, studies often comment on the significant part this plays in comparison with the actual content of what you say.

- **Remote** – written communications, including letters, reports, emails and broadly presentations (although these obviously have a spoken element).

As I've mentioned there are some principles which apply across both types of communication even if in different ways. In both cases, it's not just about what you say, it's about how you:

- **Structure it** – in a logical and persuasive way, if I follow your logic and see the evidence to support your views at the right points, I'm more likely to agree with your conclusions

- **Manage it** – in terms of emotional interaction and impact; and

- **Present it** – both:

    o   in a way that suits your audience and their requirements and preferences; and

    o   to standards that help support you in achieving the effect you desire (*Am I really going to trust this report's technical recommendations when it's riddled with spelling and grammatical errors?*).

General principles of good communications – the key dos and don'ts

Whatever the method of communication involved there are some general principles which apply in almost every situation which are summarised below. Bear these in mind if nothing else and you shouldn't go far wrong.

It's about people:

- **Relate to people and be respectful** – recognise them as individuals, use their names and be genuinely interested in them as people. Nothing will improve your communication skills more than this, almost everything else flows from it.

- **Think about their needs as a person** – we all have emotional needs such as recognition and praise, trust, a sense of belonging. See how these can be met as part of your communications. Make sure everyone has a chance to participate in the discussion.

- **Think about what they need from this exchange** – the other people involved in your exchange will be looking for something out of it by way of a specific result, so what is it and how can you help them achieve it?

- **Work to develop trust, a feeling of fairness and comfortable working relationships** – trust is essential to an effective working relationship and it and a feeling of fairness will only come from open and honest communications.

- **Think about the way they prefer to receive information** – what type (visual, spoken, written, kinaesthetic), length, or complexity of language and so on would they prefer? Then use these preferences as your guide to how you give them what they want.

It's about emotions as well as logic

- **Communicate ideas and logic to bring minds together, communicate feelings to bring people together emotionally** – and nine times out of ten emotions are stronger drivers for decision-making than logic.

- **Expressing emotions (*I feel X*) tends to feel scary, but it invites reciprocity of openness** – this binds people together emotionally, and they are also true statements of fact which are difficult to challenge.

- **Judgments are more threatening than emotions** – although judgments are usually based on how we feel, sharing emotions is less threatening and antagonistic to the person you are dealing with than making judgments (*You're wrong because you did Y*), and as an opinion they are open to challenge (*No, I'm not*).

It's about what you say

- **Have a plan** – know what you are trying to achieve, and how you are intending to go about it, before you open your mouth, pick up the phone, or start typing.

- **Be concise, focused and constructive** – marshal your arguments and deploy them one at a time in a structured way to get you to where you want to be. Someone firing out a stream of random issues as some stream of anguished consciousness with no logical structure or time to deal with each one before they are off onto the next isn't someone who's looking to resolve things, they just want to whinge.

- **Stop** – when you've said enough, don't keep on talking for the sake of talking, particularly once you've achieved your objective. Bank your win and move on.

It's about how you say it

- **Keep discussions business like** – you want to encourage constructive participation by everyone involved, generate mutual trust and motivate everyone involved, so foster listening, collaboration, positivity and people taking responsibility for actions, and avoid anything that could be construed as bullying or anti-social behaviour.

- **Keep an open mind about all suggestions** – just because you've not thought of it, doesn't mean it's wrong.

- **Be tactful** – avoid language which is going to upset your audience or get in the way of your message.

- **Simplify** – simplicity and clarity help you focus on the important core issues; always aim for simplicity and clarity, and avoid the over complex or jargon ridden.

- **Don't tell, ask** – wherever possible look for voluntary cooperation (it's about respect again) as this helps get people to buy into and actually get on and implement decisions, rather than relying on hierarchies to impose solutions which people may say yes to, but not emotionally commit to carrying through. Offer (*Have you thought about X?*) rather than suggest (*You should do Y*) advice.

- **Thank people for their input** – recognise their contribution even if you don't agree with it, and if you are not going to use it, let them know why.

- **Keep a sense of proportion and humour** – but know when humour is and is not appropriate.

- **Sometimes subtlety is more effective than directness** – particularly when you can play to people's desires to conform and be seen to behave well. David Cameron's government famously had a Nudge unit which, for example, resulted in a successful campaign to encourage tax returns with letters saying, Nine out of ten people have filed their tax returns by now.

It's not all about you: the importance of listening skills

Unless it's just me, I'd guess we've all known the feeling of being talked at by someone at some point of other and I'll leave you to make your own judgment as to how effective this will have felt as communication.

Effective communication is a two-way street and so listening is important. Getting it right establishes and maintains rapport between you and the person you are talking to, helping them feel accepted and understood. It can help them open up and give you information on their needs and feelings which can help you shape and refine your message.

It also gives you feedback on how what you are saying is being received, which again lets you modify how you structure and present it so as to achieve the result you want.

Listening in this context is about more than simply hearing. It's about actively seeking to pay attention, focusing on:

- empathising with the person who's speaking

- showing your interest in; and

- demonstrating a commitment to understanding what they have to say.

Being a poor listener by contrast means you will tend to miss information as it pops up in conversation, as well as clues and cues which would help you keep the conversation flowing smoothly and naturally. Worse still, the other person can feel frustrated, hurt or ignored as they pick up that you aren't really listening to what they have to say, aren't interested, and don't understand. Not the way to build up respect or a good working relationship.

Basic listening dos and don'ts

Poor listening tends to be due to a slightly selfish approach to the conversation, where someone is driven by too much focus on what they want out of the interaction, such as just talking about what they want to talk about, are convinced they are right and are unwilling to listen to arguments, or are simply not interested.

The starting point for good listening is to actively decide to do it and to behave accordingly (to appropriate levels depending on the situation), so do:

- Recognise this is going to be a two-way interaction and that both parties' agendas will need to be met if it's to be sucessful. So don't just focus on what you want out of the exchange, think about what they want as well.

- Seek to understand the other person's perspective and try to see things from their point of view.

- Adopt an appropriate tone for the topic of conversation and its level of seriousness.

- Give them the time and space to say what they want to say. Don't monopolise the conversation, you need to actually spend some time listening.

- Don't be selfish. Don't:
  o constantly turn the conversation back to you
  o brag, or induldge in one upmanship
  o overshare (as while it may feel good for you, it may seriously embarrass them, and this isn't all about you)
  o raise inappropriate topics (for the same reason).

- Let them have time to think if they need it. Don't necessarily rush to fill a silence, rush them to finish or seem like you need them to finish so you can speak.

- Treat them with respect. Don't:
  o interrupt them, (particularly not to pointlessly correct them on some minor technicality, or to ask distracting questions, either of which disrupts their flow)
  o cut them off
  o finish their sentences
  o prematurely summarise what you think they're going to say
  o change the subject without responding properly to what's been said.

- Pay (and be seen to pay) attention to what they say. Use appropriate body language which shows you are giving them your full attention, so shut your laptop, put down your phone and look at them when they are talking to you.

- Actively look to keep the conversation going by using appropriate short verbal encouragements and acknowledgement of points made, but when responding properly don't give too many short or one word answers. You need to give them something to work on and respond to as well.

- If a topic is being unproductive or is obviously something they do not want to talk about, move on. Similarly don't try and force a tone to the conversation, light or serious, which they are not comfortable with.

- Ask questions, but be careful to avoid going into interrogation mode. If you find yourself asking too many questions, next time you speak make a statement instead.

- Check you have understood properly what they've said by sumarising it back to them (which proves you've been listening if nothing else).

- Seriously consider whatever it is they've said. Never, ever, give the impression that you've prejudged your response, as otherwise what has been the point in having this conversation in the first place? And if you decide you need time to be able to respond properly, then say so.

- In a non-judgmental way. Don't be critical and don't be over defensive or quick to disagree.

- Be careful about when it's appropriate to offer advice or solutions, and how you go about phrasing it. *You should do X*, is very directive. *Have you thought about doing X?* is much more supportive in tone.

Sometimes it is simply difficult to be a good listener for practical reasons. I have a metal bashing factory with loud presses so everyone has to wear ear defenders while on the shop floor for health and safety reasons. As a result, when we are showing visitors or customers round, having meaningful conversations are almost impossible and these have to wait until we are back in the main offices.

It's also the case that for various reasons, some people find it more difficult than others to be good listeners. But if this is a problem you are aware of, then actively working on it by taking the steps above can make you a much better listener.

Non-verbal communication

Many studies have shown that in face-to-face communication what you say is actually less important than other factors in determining how people react.

Your tone of voice and body language can convey messages to the other person about a range of things including your:

- confidence or otherwise (and by implication, your knowledge of your subject)

- attitude towards them

- emotions; and even

- perceived degree of honesty.

So, we're going to look at the important factors of non-verbal communication including tone of voice and body language as well as the crucial element of eye contact. We'll also cover the aspect of managing the emotions of any exchange which is important given the live nature of a face-to-face interaction, but the principles of which also apply to more remote conversations such as by email.

Again, non-verbal communication is a two-way thing so while we'll be talking about how you use this to communicate you'll also be aware of others' non-verbal communication and how they impact you.

But before getting too deeply into this area, a few crucial caveats.

- **Be aware of the limited ability to control body language** – while we are very good at reading body language and tone of voice, by and large we are much less good at controlling body language as so much of it is unconscious, and it affects so many parts of our body, from the way we hold our head, our arms, our stance, to the look on our face.

    Whatever a person's desire or intent to control their body

language so as to express what they consciously want to express, unconsciously their body will be expressing how they feel anyway.

Whatever front you are putting on you can get leakage where the reality of how you are feeling seeps out from behind the appearance you are trying to give, which can undermine trust in your sincerity (check out YouTube for videos on how to tell a real from a fake smile, for example).

And the further the two sets of behaviours are apart, the worse and more obvious the leakage will be.

So, try to make sure that both your body language and tone of voice act to reinforce what you are saying and don't work against it.

- **Read body language and tone as a group of signals** – following on from the point above when you're assessing someone else's body language, don't just focus on one thing that they may be trying to present, or where they may adopt an inappropriate stance for a while without it meaning anything. Instead try to look at all the non-verbal clues you are receiving as a package to see the overall message you are being given.

- **Be aware of individual and cultural differences** – different cultures will have different gestures, customs and expectations about behaviour, so ensure you take these into account when trying to assess how an individual feels about something.

  By the same token, you should also seek to moderate your non-verbal communication to suit your audience, taking into account their age, emotional state and culture.

- **Realise that your body language interacts with the way you are feeling** – ever had someone tell you to smile and it will feel better? Well they're actually probably right as your body language is not simply a one-way street directed by how you feel.

  How you feel can be affected by your body, so on the *Fake it till you make it principle*, one way of getting over nerves about say, an interview, is to adopt the stance and mannerisms appropriate to self-confidence. If you act the part by smiling and holding yourself in a confident way, this will translate back into improved actual feelings of confidence.

Having said all the above, it remains the case that having appropriate body language is critical to being perceived as engaged and enabling successful listening, so when dealing with someone in person remember to:

- **Always face the speaker** – turn your whole body towards them and lean forwards to show you are interested in them.

- **Have an open stance** – no crossed arms or defensive postures, and if possible, sit or stand so there aren't any objects between you (no hiding behind that desk).

- **Don't come across as too aggressive** – being too dominant and assertive can be as bad as too withdrawn, defensive or disinterested.

- **Make and keep a good level of eye contact** – again to signal they have your full attention, this is a key social signal that you are engaged with the person you are speaking to which we will come back to below.

- **Keep an appropriate expression** – which will obviously depend on the nature of what is being discussed.

- **Mirror for empathy** – if you adopt a similar stance to the person you are talking to this can lead to feelings of empathy. But don't overdo this as it's easy to spot and if done badly can make the other person feel extremely uncomfortable.

- **Be aware of people's personal space** – we all have a distance around us which we regard as being our personal space and the distance we want to keep from others. While this has some flexibility dependent on circumstances, we are very sensitive to people who come too close without permission and invade it. If you notice people tending to physically drift backwards while you are talking to them, this is a sign you may just be getting too close (as your sense of personal space is tighter than theirs) and you might want to try to take a step back.

- **Be very careful about physical contact** – following on from above, people's attitudes to and tolerance of physical contact will vary hugely, dependent on personal nature, cultural background and the current emotional circumstances. So be very careful about initiating any physical contact outside of the very formalised rituals of, for example, shaking hands on meeting, until you are sure about what is called for.

However in situations (such as a funeral) or environments where physical contact is part of the culture (hugs and air kisses are just the norm in some places) then you need to participate, as otherwise you may be felt to be cold, standoffish, or even snooty.

Body language is an area where it's worth practising so try videoing yourself while talking to people and watching how you act. Even better, have a friend watch you and give you feedback on what you do well and where you have room for improvement, as seeing ourselves as others see us is a very difficult trick to pull off but vitally important for developing yourself in this area.

Things to look for include:

- **smiling** – either too little, or too much

- **facial expression** – appropriate to the subject and speaker

- **eye contact** – failing to make or keep it

- **poor posture** – defensive closed or distanced in stance (crossed arms and legs), or disengaged (slouching or head down)

- **tone of voice** – being too loud or too quiet, speaking too quickly or too flatly

- **positioning** – too close or too far away

- **distraction** – failing to pay attention, looking around or at your phone.

Don't try to do too much at first. Concentrate on whatever your main weakness seems to be, practising improvements in front of the mirror and in non-threatening social sitiations so you build up your confidence and experience before you try rolling them out at work or using them on your boss.

Eye contact

Many people have a particular difficulty with eye contact as for anyone who's shy it can feel challenging or distracting while you try to think about what you want to say. Unfortunately however, failing to make or keep an appropriate level of eye contact is often interpreted as at best a lack of interest (*as your attention is obviously elsewhere*), and at worst as being untrustworthy or dishonest (*as you can't or won't look me in the eye*).

Before starting to work on this area specifically do however check how much eye contact you are making as it might be more than you think.

It may also be that other aspects of your body language are either more important for you to work on, or compensate for any deficiencies in eye contact.

I know for example I'm pretty poor at making eye contact, in part because I have dreadful eyesight and effectively only one working eye, so I have to make a conscious effort to work at this when I'm speaking to people. In response I compensate by working on other areas of my body language which I find easier to control such as smiling, posture, and tone of voice.

If you have a problem with eye contact it's unlikely that you will be able to change what are probably the habits of a lifetime overnight, so you will need to gradually train yourself to be more comfortable with it.

To practise developing better eye contact:

- Start with situations where you are the listener rather than the speaker, so you have more capacity to concentrate part of your attention on actively maintaining eye contact. When you are speaking you have lots more to think about so your eyes will have a greater tendency to wander.

- Realise you don't actually have to look them directly in the eye, certainly not all the time. If you look somewhere in that direction they usually can't tell you are actually focusing on their forehead.

- Practise on people you are comfortable with to start with. Eye contact can be challenging in all senses of the word and so it's always going to be more difficult to maintain it with somone intimidating than with someone who's friendly, so again it's about building your skills and confidence until you can look anyone in the eye, however scary they may be.

- Aim for short bursts of eye contact to start with. You can always build up to longer periods later.

Making persuasive arguments, how structuring what you say helps you get what you want

We've covered a lot of ground about how to go about saying things so as to best pitch them to your audience in a way they'll be receptive to. But, no matter how much they are prepared to listen, you still need to structure your arguments in a way that will convince them.

This is most obvious when thinking about say, writing a report, and so in this section we'll tend to be talking about this type of communication in order to illustrate the principles, but in reality, the underlying logic also applies to verbal and face-to-face communication as well, so you may want to try to bear them in mind when you are talking on the hoof.

We're briefly going to cover four techniques:

- **Monroe's motivated sequence** – a five-step approach to structuring an argument so as to persuade people to take action (which unsurprisingly has found its way in various forms into a lot of sales and marketing processes. Watch out for it next time someone tries to sell you something, or you see a cheesy advert on TV.)

- **The inverted pyramid** – a classic structure used in journalism to tell a story in an easily digestible way.

- **The rule of threes** – a standard approach to creating an effective professional report and getting your message across; and

- The old fashioned **rhetorical triangle** – the convincing language of logos, pathos and ethos.

After which there's a short section giving some tips for making successful presentations.

Monroe's motivated sequence

Developed in the 1930s by Alan H Monroe, this is simply a structured five-step approach to organising any speech or document in a way which leads people to want to take action:

1. **Attention** – to get people to take action, firstly you need them to be listening to what you have to say which means you need to get their attention. You grab this by using something dramatic and involving which could be a shocking statistic, assertion, example or story.

   People across the UK are due X Billion in PPI compensation by the banks.

2. **Need** – that's all very well but there are lots of shocking things and problems out there. What will motivate someone to take action is that they have a relevant need, which is significant to them personally, and which is not going to go away by itself. Show how the problem relates to your specific audience and why they personally need to act.

   If you had a bank loan you could have thousands of pounds in compensation waiting for your claim.

3. **Satisfaction** – and hey, you know what? You've got the very solution they're looking for. But don't just say it, demonstrate it by using specific examples that your audience can use to resolve the issue.

   Our free PPI check will tell you in seconds how much you could be owed and how to claim it.

4. **Visualisation** – enable your audience to see what will happen when they take action and what life will be like for them afterwards once they have (and for real impact show what it will be like if they don't).

   Mrs X of Y (pictured smiling happily with a large cheque) checked and claimed £15,000. Our free claims service can do all the work for you so your cheque will be with you within a month.

5. **Call to action** – finally, spell out the exact steps they need to take, personally, now, to take action to solve their problem.

   But hurry, the FSA is considering bringing an end to all claims soon so don't miss out. Call or click here now for your free PPI check.

This approach has a number of advantages in that it:

- feels to your audience when done properly as though it is directed at their specific problem (as you have defined it), giving them the feeling that you have been listening, understand and care about them

- makes you look like an expert as you have not only defined the problem but provided the solution and the means to implement it; and

- is action focused, structured around and towards what the audience can actually do (particularly important if your audience's initial reaction is that there's nothing they can do).

Inverted pyramid

A good journalist is someone who can both report a story quickly and clearly, and in doing so grab the reader's attention so they want to find out more.

The classic journalistic approach to writing known as the inverted pyramid uses a summary first-explain later methodology to achieve just this effect as you will see by looking at any newspaper.

Writing in this style involves telling the relevant parts of the story right at the outset, in order of importance, giving a summary by way of a taster which then encourages people to go on to read the detail which underlies it:

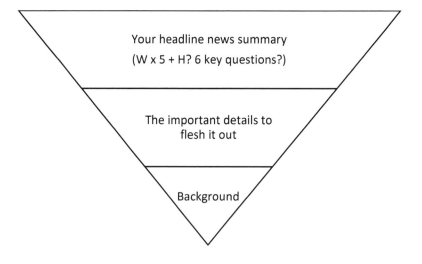

Busy executives are just that, busy, so they often don't have the time or inclination to want to absorb huge amounts of detail while trying to spot the important facts or conclusions to be drawn, although they may need this available to check what is being presented to them or drill down/deep dive into an area of interest.

Hence most reports will start with an executive summary encapsulating on one or two pages the key points (takeaways) a reader should learn or appreciate from the document.

You can see how applicable the inverted pyramid approach is to writing at work as it is:

- **effective** in ensuring that the key information is clearly summarised right at the start; and

- **efficient** in saving your readers' time as they don't have to wade through reams of information and data to get to the key points (whilst the backing information is available for reference if required)

- **impressive** as it shows your ability to extract and present the key information in a concise and informative way so your reader gets it right away.

Writing using this approach is a process which involves:

- **Selecting the key points the reader needs to know, whether information or conclusions** – you need to assess:
    - what are the most critical messages you want to get across in whatever you are writing
    - what is the shortest way of sumarising each of them; and then
    - rank them in order from most to least important.

- **Frontloading your document with your resulting summary** – you need to limit the space for your opening summary so that it really is a summary and something which can be easily read. It should only be two or three paragraphs, or half a dozen bullet points at most, starting with the most important and then working down in order, so that someone who just reads the summary will get all the key points of your message.

- **Deciding how many of the six key questions to cover** – the six key questions in any story are what, who, where, when, why, and how, but trying to cover all of these in your summary is probbaly impossible, so again it's a matter of prioritising what's important which in many cases looks like:

  o **what and who** usually need to be in there otherwise your reader doesn't know what you are talking about,

  o **when and where** may or may not be of critical relevance so may need to be in the summary or can be relegated to the body of the report; while

  o **why and how** are the detail which should be relegated to the text, if not appendices.

- **KISS (Keep it Simple Stupid)** – always use normal everday language your audience will understand. And on the same basis don't use jargon as you are automatically excluding anyone who's not familiar with the terms you are using.

- **Provide the bulk of your report** – having created your opening summary, the temptation can then be to stuff everything else you have into the body of your report. While the body of your document is the place to expand on and set out your argument and provide your information, it does still need to be properly structured so as to be easily digestible by a reader and to clearly support your summarised conclusions.

- **Use appendices** – when in doubt, relegate data or any other large 'stand alone' pieces to an appendix, where the reader can access them if required, but where they do not get in the way of the flow of your argument.

There are however some risks to be aware of in using this style:

- A logical argument might typically go A => B => C which provides an explanatory structure a reader can follow and can help with convincing them C is the answer. The inverted pyramid approach by contrast may well start with C since the answer is the important thing, followed perhaps by X and Y as the next most important conclusions, while the causal chain of A and B to support these conclusions may follow some way much further down the chain.

- Similarly, the style allows readers to read the summary knowing they will be getting the key points, whilst making the body and detail of the report almost an optional extra (hence the need to make sure your opening summary really does cover everything they absolutely have to know).

- You may actively want to lead people through a process, (such as Monroe's motivated sequence above) where whilst you want to hook their attention at the start, you don't want to give away your whole pitch right at the outset.

- And some readers may simply be more comfortable with a more traditional story approach and expect to see a beginning, a middle and an end, in that order, so they know where they are.

So where explanation by way of a logical exposition, or caveats, or conveying detailed information are critical to what you need to communicate, the inverted pyramid may not be the most appropriate structure for the body of your report (although it may still be the best way to compile your executive summary).

What I tell you three times is true – report writing for beginners and the rule of three

As mentioned above, a traditional story telling approach has a three-act structure of a beginning, a middle and an end, where events follow a logical order, (often chronological in a story), where A leads to B which results in C. This is something everybody will be familiar with and helps your points to flow naturally from each other, and if you want to make your report easy to follow then it makes sense to use this format where your audience will know what to expect.

It does however also mean you have to think carefully through what you want to say and arrange to set it out in an appropriately logical order. If your report runs A, B, F, D, Z, Q, Y, I'm probably going to get confused and may even give up long before I've got to C.

This three-part approach also allows you to get your message across to your audience three times as the process of writing the body of your report follows a three-act structure, in that you have:

- **The introduction** – where you tell your audience what you are going to tell them – setting their expectations about what they are going to read and priming them to follow your logic

- **The body** – where you tell them what you are telling them – delivering your evidence and arguments to convince them; and

- **The conclusions** (and importantly for generating actions, your recommendations) – where you tell them what you've told them – showing how you draw the evidence together into the outcome presented.

However, you've not quite finished, as only now should you look to summarise your report into your executive summary which should ideally fit onto a single page.

When you are actually writing your report, you need to keep in mind the general best practise points covered earlier in this chapter but in particular you need to ensure you make it:

- **Relevant** – be clear about what you are intending to achieve by writing this report, is it simply to inform or is it intended to convince or generate specific actions? Knowing what you are trying to achieve at the outset is really very useful in helping you do what you want to do.

- **Targeted** – be clear about who you are writing for, and write for them in a way and language they will feel comfortable with and understand.

- **Short** – people have busy lives and ever shorter attention spans so your report should be just long enough to do what it needs to do, but no longer. Just the sight of a doorstop report is enough to put some people off ever opening it.

- **Comprehensive** – you need to cover what you need to cover, so give some thought to what questions, objections or challenges might be raised to your data, findings or conclusions and deal with them within your report.

  It can be difficult to see the issues in something you've produced so try having a friend or colleague give it a critical or cold review where they play devil's advocate and argue against your points. This can be a painful experience but better to have them pick apart any holes or weaknesses in your draft so you can fix them in private, than let the big wide world or your boss do it in public.

- **Attractive** – how your report looks is also important to how easy it is to read so use:

- o Clear headers and sub headers to indicate your key topics.

- o Bullet points and numbered lists to call out related groups of key points.

- o Graphs, images, diagrams and tables to present data or flows of ideas (in colour if that's practical and affordable).

- o Appendices to clear clutter. Be ruthless with data and move as much of the bulk of information out of the body of your report and into appendices as possible. Your audience doesn't usually need to read all the tables of data as they go through what you've written, other than possibly to check a reference or a note. They're trusting you've done that in order to produce your report, so get them out of the way.

- **Right** – your report is going to be a very permanent and public (to your intended audience) thing and so it's something on which fairly or unfairly, people may be judging you for some time to come.

Don't let basic errors in, for example spelling, formatting, or punctuation detract from the thought and effort you have put into it. As covered in the next section you should always review and revise it thoroughly before ever signing it off for publication.

Make sure you have done your research properly. Double and triple check your data to make sure it's right, and always annotate it with reference back to the source material and date so it's clear where it came from.

For anything of any importance I'd always recommend reading it out loud to yourself, and again, asking a friend to give it a critical review to spot any errors or question anything which seems unclear or ambiguous.

The rhetorical triangle

People have been trying to convince other people through speech and writing for thousands of years, and the principles and techniques of rhetoric were established in classical times.

One of these concepts going back to Aristotle (bet you didn't think he'd be showing up) is the rhetorical triangle. This says there are three basic types of appeal and any argument should be made on the basis of using one or more of these in the combination best suited to both the argument, and your relationship to your audience.

The three types are:

- **Logos** – is your appeal to reason based on facts and logic (*You should do X because of facts Y and Z*).

- **Pathos** – is your emotional appeal to your audience (*You should do X because you know it's the right thing to do*). If you can get them feeling emotional, then you can get them to take emotionally driven decisions.

- **Ethos** – is your appeal based on your credibility, character or authority (*You should do X because you trust me as a person, or you know my track record and believe I know what I'm doing, or recognise I'm the world's leading expert in Y and Z*).

The strongest, most effective arguments are usually based on a combination of all three approaches, but you can mix and match combinations to see what works best, on what topic, with which audience.

You can hopefully see for example how a strong ethos (*I'm clearly an expert so you can trust what I say on this topic*) would help support your logos (*Here's the facts and the conclusion you should draw from them*) in convincing an audience and overcoming any scepticism about what they are being told.

If you can then add on the emotional element of some pathos (*And I've lived with or been affected by X personally, so I know why it's so important*), you are building an argument which people will find difficult to resist.

Presentations

One area of communication which can cause great concern for people is anything involving making a presentation or other forms of public speaking (I used to be physically sick before standing up in front of people at times). However, there is nothing like success in this field for building both your confidence and reputation so it's well worth making the effort to do it well.

In addition to thinking through how you are going to organise your material using the techniques and approaches already discussed, some tips for ensuring a successful presentation are:

- **Be prepared** – make sure you know who's organising what kit. Get there early, get set up and make sure everything works. Five minutes of frantic fiddling with a laptop or a projector while your audience is getting restless in their seats is not the way you want to begin.

   So make sure:

   o   you know who's supplying the equipment required and you've confirmed it's going to be there and available

   o   your presentation is loaded; you know how to switch on and off any equipment you need and how to move between slides when you need to

   o   you know where you are speaking from and your notes, props or any other equipment you need such as pens or a flipchart are to hand for when you need them

   o   if the venue is so large that you need a microphone check that it's working and again you know how to use it; and finally

   o   you can see a clock to keep an eye on your timings as you go.

- **Be readable** – keep your slides brief and legible from anywhere in the room. Think 6 x 6 (maximum of six lines with no more than six words per line) in a large, plain and dark font with strong contrast against its background. As someone who's blind as a bat my heart sinks when a presenter uses that dread phrase, *Now you may not be able to see this as it's rather small...* One of these days I'm going to stick my hand up and ask, *Well why have you put it in then?*

- **Be entertaining and add value** – don't just read your slides. Apart from the fact this tends to make you face the screen, usually showing your back to your audience as you do so, you will find that most of your audiences have actually learnt to read for themselves a while ago. They will therefore find it boring as you are not adding anything to what they can read for themselves. Remember they are here to listen to you talk, not just to read your slides, and so you are there to talk with your slides supporting what you say, not the other way round.

- **Be creative and interesting** – use pictures, images and diagrams. Remember some people will prefer these as ways to absorb information anyway and this will have the added advantage that you can't just read them out even if you want to, you have to describe and interpret them.

- **Be confident** – remember your audience will generally be supportive and will want you to succeed. They will usually be sympathetic as many people actively dislike public speaking and they will simply be glad you are up there and not them.

- **Be practised** – don't overdo it and over-rehearse, you want to be natural, but doing a run through once or twice will make you more confident in what you say and how you link it to your slides, as well as being aware of your timings so you don't overrun your allotted slot.

- **Be approachable** – invest in and engage with your audience emotionally:

  o Smile (I draw smiley faces on my notes to remind me as I go along).

  o Be confident, this is your show, these people are here to listen to you speak and the next however long belongs to you.

  o Introduce yourself, let people know who you are, why you are going to be talking to them, and why it matters to you, not just what you are talking about.

  o Set your ground rules. Do you want to have questions as you go through (keeps it interesting but only if you are confident you can wing it) or at the end (more controllable)? Let people know.

  o But remember, successful communication isn't a one-way street, so make friends with your audience. Ask them questions, get a show of hands, do whatever's appropriate to get them involved and actively participating in what you are saying, not simply sitting there and passively listening. This can be as simple as checking with them every so often, looking to confirm that people are still with you, have understood what's been covered so far, and are happy to move on to the next topic.

o Make it interesting to listen to in terms of how you say it, not just what you are saying. Vary your tone, volume, and emphasis as you go through. Don't think about it as presenting, think of it as acting. Your presentation should be a showcase for your passion, expertise, or commitment to whatever it is you are speaking about where you want them to become emotionally involved and invested in what you are saying. Put yourself in the audience's shoes. If you don't sound as though you are interested in what you have to say, then why should they be?

- **Be clear about what they can expect** – tell them there'll be notes and handouts given out at the end, or they'll spend all their time frantically scribbling as you talk. But make it at the end; if you give slides out at the start people will flick through them while you're still introducing yourself, decide they know what you are going to say before you've finished your introduction and will zone out for the rest of your talk.

The importance of presentation – getting the basics right so as to not to let yourself down

There are two main reasons why the presentation of what you write is important:

- the impression it gives of your professionalism; and

- its effectiveness of achieving what you want.

And in practise, the two of these are linked as it's not just what you say, but how you are perceived to say it which helps make your communications effective.

For example, the communications sent out by a business are critical to the impression formed by customers and prospective customers of the organisation. So yes, your boss may be very hot on the importance of grammar, spelling and punctuation, but it's not just for the fun of it. It's because what the customer sees is very important to how they judge whether the organisation is any good or not.

If you get a sloppy letter full of mistakes from an organisation, how confident are you likely to be that when it comes to it, they will actually do a good job? And if not, why would you hire them?

Also bear in mind that you are likely to be communicating with people from many different generations, who may have been educated with very different attitudes to the use of language in business communications and standards they expect to see. Leaving all questions of level of formality aside for a moment, as this is another issue you'll need to think about, you do need to expect to be judged on your use of spelling and grammar.

Assumptions and completeness

One of the key things to think about when issuing any communication is the extent to which it needs to act as a stand-alone document so that someone coming to it for the first time can understand it. You therefore need to consider:

- who might see it; and

- how much information do you need to give?

Often a document such as a business plan or a forecast may have some important assumptions which are critical to understanding it and you need to ensure these are communicated so a reader can make sense of what's being said. All too often I see business forecasts being issued as tables of numbers with no explanation as to what the guesses are that lie behind them.

If my bank manager calls up wanting to discuss my overdraft with me I might send them a forecast which shows I'm planning to spend £2 on Friday and expecting to bank £1,000,000 on Monday which will more than clear my borrowings.

How is my bank manager going to feel about this? Pretty pleased that I'm going to pay off the overdraft they've been worried about? Looking forward to selling me investment advice on how to look after my money?

Possibly.

Because it all depends, and without any details of the assumptions underlying these numbers it's actually very difficult for them to tell anything.

If I'm planning to spend £2 on the bus fare to my solicitors so I can collect the cheque they have arranged for my £1,000,000 legacy from dear departed Aunty Mabel, then yes they're likely to be feeling calm about my overdraft for the rest of the week.

If I'm planning to spend the £2 on buying a lottery ticket for Saturday and the £1,000,000 is what I'm expecting to win, then I'd expect them to be much less relaxed.

If you are communicating with someone, think about what the person needs to know to see, understand and accept the whole picture you want to convey. Don't send them half a story.

Think about how it reads cold

The other question you should ask yourself is how it might be interpreted, as anything written always runs the risk of being seen out of context.

If I'm the Finance Director of a business specialising in supplying business information and reports, I could write this to Peter, the Managing Director:

> Hi Pete
>
> We need to worry about insolvency – cash flow test, not being able to pay bills when due; and balance sheet, liabilities exceeding assets.
>
> Regards
>
> Mark
>
> Finance Director

Now let's say you caught sight of this email and read it without knowing anything about the context. What would you think I'm talking about? I'm the Finance Director and I'm telling the Managing Director we need to worry about insolvency, cash flow and not being able to pay bills when they are due. It doesn't sound too good, does it? If this email was then circulated amongst the business's staff, its suppliers, its customers or its bankers, the consequences could be very serious.

However, if instead I actually wrote:

> Hello Peter [Use of a more formal introduction and his proper name makes this a more business-like communication.]
>
> Further to our conversation about developing a business liquidity review and reporting product, I have given some thought to the areas we need to be thinking about. [This introduction puts the communication in context.]
>
> Being able to identify insolvency issues and risks in companies being reviewed is likely to be a key concern of users of our reports, in respect of which the two areas we will need to ensure are covered are the ability to consider:
>
> - the cash flow test of companies not being able to pay their bills when these fall due; and
>
> - the balance sheet test of where their liabilities exceed their assets.
>
> Regards
>
> Mark
>
> Finance Director

Now it's clear that what I'm actually talking about is the design of a new report and the information it's going to need to contain. So there's no need for anyone who reads it to worry about anything at all.

Prepare, prepare, prepare

All the general rules of communication we've covered so far obviously apply here, whether you are writing a letter, a report or an email, so keep it professional in tone, clear and concise, appropriately structured, and remember to think about the audience you are looking to reach.

- **Personalise your opening** – you are communicating person to person so make it clear you are thinking about them as a person.

- **Close it off properly** – sign off appropriately at the end. On email set up standard signatures, as in any business communications you will need to include some important information about the organisation you are working for (the Business Names Act for example sets out some legal requirements for disclosure on all company stationery).

- **Take your time to draft** – anything that's important I tend to draft in Word first and only cut and paste it to an email once I am happy with it, which also avoids the risk of firing it off by accident in a half-finished state.

- **Signpost and structure** – help people find their way through what you are writing. Use titles and subtitles to flag up key topics, and use bullet points or numbering for lists, and keep detail to clearly structured appendices.

- **Always reference** – so it's clear where detail can be found or comes from. You are writing to communicate to busy people, you're not creating some kind of treasure hunt.

- **Ensure what you've said is clear** – Read what you have written out loud. By doing so you will soon find where it doesn't flow or is confusing. But for this to work you really do need to read it out loud to yourself properly, however odd that may feel at first. If you just read it silently in your head, you'll find you read what you expect to see, not what's actually there. If in doubt about clarity, structure or tone, ask a colleague to read it through for you and get their feedback on what does and doesn't work.

- **Think about the length** – make sure you have enough in there to answer all points or questions which might get raised, but not too much.

- **Make it self-contained** – At the same time, ensure it's the truth, the whole truth and everything you need to understand the truth. As far as possible everthing you say should be able to be read as a stand alone document (as you can't always rely on anyone who ever sees it having access to all the other supporting documenation with which to make sense of it).

  Obviously for practical reasons in many cases you can't include all the relevant data, correspondence, papers and so on, so in these cases always ensure you refer to whatever it is a reader needs to be aware of to understand the position so they at least know where to find what they need.

- Specific email issues include:

  o **Don't treat email as different** – your business email is a business communication. Treat it as such and keep it formal. Would you really use an emoticon in a normal business letter?

  o **Use the subject line effectively** – it's your correspondent's introduction to what you are writing (and may be necessary to get them to open it in the first place) and also very useful when searching through your emails for a relevant item so make sure it reflects the topic and content of the email.

  o **Whatever you put in an email will be there forever** – so be careful what you say, about who.

  o **Keep an orderly archive** – you never know when you are going to need to be able to refer to that old email again.

Check, check, check, and oh yes, check

- **Check your facts** – when you are sending something out in writing it has a natural air of authority and your readers will be expecting you to provide them with quality information. Nothing damages your credibility quicker than circulating something that's just plain wrong, as people won't automatically trust whatever you send thereafter.

- **Check you have copied information across correctly so it is right when it gets to the reader**– you might have the right facts in your notes, but you need to make sure they are accurately incorporated into what reaches the reader, particularly if a document goes through a number of drafts. When I started out as a trainee accountant a dull but vital part of the job was calling over accounts, which involved one trainee reading out the accounts and all the numbers from one draft copy to another, whose job it was to check they had been correctly copied over into the next.

- **Check your grammar** – spell check, grammar check, punctuation. Your computer will do these for you, so let it, but your computer is not infallible so do read it yourself. In a work of any size such as a book like this, it's not uncommon to still find some errors even after having had a number of reviews and professional proof reading.

- **Check for usual gramatical errors** – you are not a grocer so always check for and eliminate grocers' apostrophes, they are something that will drive some readers absolutely nuts. Also you're not writing in German, so don't sprinkle your sentences with Capitalised Words just because they seem important. Capital letters are used in specific circumstances.

- **Check your sense and readability** – but then also read it for sense (preferably out loud as already discussed), and if it's really important, get a friend to read it too. Your computer can also generate a series of readability scores so you can check how complex your writing style is.

- **Check it will be understood** – is your language understandable?

- **Check your addressees** – who are you sending it to? Who are you copying in (and why? Do they really need to see it?).

  What order are you putting your addressees in? If it's not alphabetical then people may assume the order is in some kind of importance. (Who might be upset by this?)

  Blind copying (bcc) means sending something to someone without others being aware you've done so. Be very careful using this. Always consider what will happen if the others find out later.

- **Check you've been received** – don't always assume an email in particular has gone through, it may have been marked as spam or you may have an error in the address you are using, especially if it's the first time you've sent something. If it's important, check, or use a read receipt. If you find your emails to someone are bouncing, speak to them about it. It may be there's a size limit on the attachments they can receive, or certain file types are blocked, or they simply need to add you to their white list to allow your mails to come through.

- **Check your attachments** – if you've referred to a document or a spreadsheet, have you actually remembered to attach it? It's such an easy mistake to make that my email system now asks me if I've forgotten something if I use the word attach in an email. Even so I still have to send the, Oops, sorry I forgot to attach, apology far too regularly for comfort.

Does your attachment have a meaningful title so the user will know what it's about?

Is it in a format they will actually be able to open?

Do you want them to be able to open and manipulate the data, or do you want it to be locked, either password protected, or turned into a pdf?

- **Check your attachments are right** – spreadsheets in particular need to be checked to make sure they add up both across and down (checking they cast and cross cast) as it's very easy for lines to be inserted or formulas not to be updated resulting in tables which simply don't add up. And ensure you've set out any assumptions needed to understand them.

- **Check you have the right version** – as documents or spreadsheets are developed and passed berween people for comment and amendment, you will often end up with a series of versions. So when you are producing your final report, or sending that email, always check to make sure you have the right version of the document or spreadsheet, otherwise mass confusion will ensue.

- **Check your trail** – very often you may be responding to an email you've received and as they bounce between people they build up a trail of prior messages which can contain confidential information. To avoid the sort of problem I described in my introduction to this chapter, always check to see what's buried in this trail before simply hitting forward or reply on an email.

- **Check what you are giving away** – email in particular is not a private medium from a technical point of view. From a practical point of view this is also relevant for any written communication in that you cannot normally physically control who any letter, report or email will eventually be shown to.

So always consider what the implications would be of what you are sending being shared more widely.

Do you need to include a disclaimer in case people look to rely on what you say (often known as boilerplate language)?

Do you need to have a confidentiality agreement in place to control who is supposed to have access to it?

If you find yourself writing things that need the words Without Prejudice or Subject To Contract in the subject line then this is something you need to be thinking very carefully about.

- **Check what you can and can't use** – this applies espcially to images. Just because you've seen something on the internet does not mean it's available for use. Copyright laws still apply and some of the image libraries are now going after unauthorised users aggressively.

It's a widespread problem and I've had experienced professionals who frankly should have known better, provide me with material for publication which has included images harvested from the internet and which could have left us open to being sued if we'd used them.

Don't get your employer sued. It's not a good career move. If you need images buy them online from reputable sources such as Shutterstock.

8   Managing your career

I once made a huge career mistake. I had been looking unsuccessfully to leave my existing firm for over two years, and so when a job in industry came up, I just took it, even though it meant upping sticks and moving to the other end of the country.

I was recruited in by someone else who'd only recently joined and I soon realised it was case of out of the frying pan and into the fire, in that my (and it turned out my recruiter's) face didn't fit, and so within two years we were both out of the door.

I think we both knew we were on the way out for a while before it happened, and a few months before we each got the heave ho, we were talking and he said to me: *You're bright, you'll end up doing what you want to do.*

At the time I really wasn't so sure, and then later when I was made redundant while living in an area where I had absolutely no work or professional connections I'd have said he was mad. But you know what? As it turns out he was absolutely right, about the doing what I want to bit at least (opinion is probably divided about the bright part).

Nowadays I have a career where I write (which is what I always wanted to do), I buy businesses in difficulty to turn around and run on my own account (which is what I'd always wanted my career to be about) and I'm my own boss (which is the type of freedom I've always wanted, as well as just being a practical necessity as by now I'm completely unemployable).

Am I rich? Have I got security?

No, not in the slightest.

I eat what I catch and sometimes it's a very precarious existence. I have had lean periods where I've earned next to nothing for months (no years) on end, and I've had businesses go down into which I've put money and lost the lot. By and large my ex-colleagues who stayed in the profession, or who have made secure careers in industry have all made far more money and have had a far more comfortable existence than I've achieved out on my own.

But am I doing what I wanted to do? Absolutely.

This is a book about your first year in the workplace, it's not a book about career planning, there are plenty of those out there which can help you make those critical life choices. So, we are going to keep this basic and cover some foundations you should be thinking about, whatever you decide you eventually want to do (and hint, it might well not be what you are doing now).

In this chapter, we'll therefore look at:

- The need to recognise the issues and take responsibility for managing your career, together with some pointers as to how what's required to progress in your career may change over time.

- How to go about laying the foundations of managing your career (even if you've no clue what it's going to be yet), by beginning to build brand 'You' through how you present yourself, your social media profile, having a hinterland, and starting to work on developing your support network, where it's never too early to network, so long as you do it right.

- Understanding what attributes and attitudes are going to help take you forward, by looking at what employers see as the key characteristics and traits of exceptional employees and the need for continuous personal development and learning, and investing in your training and skills.

- As well as that crucial topic, of actually deciding what you do want to do and some basic self-assessment and career planning approaches you need to consider.

Why you need to manage your career

I'm sorry if this is going to sound depressing, but if you are reading this book at the outset of your working life, the likelihood is you are going to be working for the next 40 to 50 years or so. Realising this however means that I'd suggest you can try and make it as:

- enjoyable

- rewarding (financially and otherwise); and

- successful as possible

by doing something that you want to do and advancing as far as you can in your chosen field (as 40 to 50 years of doing something you don't like, never wanted to do, and which leaves you unfulfilled, is not a route to personal happiness – see Maslow's hierarchy of needs in Chapter 9 if you need an explanation).

But achieving this isn't likely to come about simply by happy accident.

If you want something to happen, the first thing you need is a plan, so coming from a business background, I'd encourage you to think of yourself as a small business.

You have skills you want to sell and services you want to provide, into a market of employers, clients, customers and consumers.

So you need a business plan for the business of you.

And you need to be your own managing director, in charge of your plan of where you want to go and the steps you need to take to get there.

It's your career, it's your life. No one is ever going to (or ought to) care about that more than you. If you want it to be a success then you need to take responsibility for it, starting right now.

I took a gap year before I went to university and then another year working afterwards which was intended to help me save to do a masters degree. As it happened in both of these jobs I found myself working as bag man to directors of businesses that were in some difficulty, and the second of them actually went into insolvency while I was there.

The first however was being run by a managing director who'd been brought in to turn the business around, and as there were only eight of us in the head office I got to see him at quite close quarters. And what I saw was someone who'd just turned 40, was being paid extremely well for doing a job that seemed interesting and exciting, with a house in Florida, a townhouse in Pimlico, an attractive blonde girlfriend and his and hers matching Mercedes.

And so as an impressionable 17-year-old I thought:

o   That looks fun.

o   That looks rewarding (yes, there are deeper puddles than me).

o   I'm quite bright; and so

o   Why don't I do that?

And that was literally how I first decided I wanted to be a company doctor or turnaround specialist.

But how could I go about it? How could I get to the point where people would hand me businesses in difficulty to run and restore to health, and pay me handsomely (I hoped) to do so?

So I sat down and thought and came up with a plan. I decided there were probably a number of experiences and ticks in the boxes I would need to achieve over the first ten years or so of my career so as to become the sort of person who could get that type of job, and with my career shopping list in mind, I set out to obtain:

- **A business qualification** – so I'd know something about business (having done a social sciences degree), and I took an MBA.

- **Financial expertise** – so I could understand and manage the numbers, and having completed my MBA I joined an accountancy firm and qualified as a chartered accountant.

- **Experience in running and selling businesses in difficulty** – so I could practise doing what I wanted to do on other people's companies. Towards the end of my accountancy training I managed a transfer into the firm's insolvency department where we dealt with distressed businesses and were appointed as receivers and administrators to run and sell them.

- **Overseas or multi-cultural experience** – so I'd be seen to have familiarity with international business, so I managed to achieve an international secondment within the firm where I spent two and a half years overseas, going out to manage the turnaround and sale of one of the largest private sector companies, helping to manage winding up a failed bank, and setting up a new practice area; and

- **Banking experience** – as banks tended to be one of the key drivers of this type of business restructuring, and I managed to obtain a secondment into one of the main clearing banks' business support units.

Meanwhile, I'd always been open and told my bosses that a career in turnaround was what I was working towards. So, when my firm decided to set up a pilot turnaround unit which needed a project manager, the partner I worked for put my name forward and I got the job. Which then meant over the next two years, one of the key parts of my role was to help conduct first interviews with every turnaround professional we could find across the UK to recruit a panel of experts, giving me in effect a series of three-hour masterclasses every week in how all the established players went about their work.

Was my plan naïve? Yes, in the extreme at the outset, but as I worked through it I refined and learnt as I went.

Was I lucky? Yes.

But was I lucky because I had a plan and knew what I was looking for? Well, yes.

Having ideas about what you want to do is a good start, but that's all it is.

To make it happen you need to take action, and have the determination to see it through to success, whatever comes your way.

Your first job won't be your last, but it's up to you to make it a real step on the way to doing what you really want to do.

What does your job require and how will this change?

One of the things you will need to recognise to manage your career in the longer term is that what's important in your role at work will change as you gain seniority in almost any organisation.

To start with your focus will be very much on doing the job, but even at this stage you will still need to have some focus on managing people whether that's your relationships with your co-workers or your boss, and everyone within a business whether they recognise it or not has a responsibility for helping to sell and develop the business in the way they conduct themselves as its representatives.

At the outset, your skills will tend to be quite general as you won't have had the chance to pick up deep expertise in an area, but as you train and develop you will start to specialise and will be judged on how well you do your job.

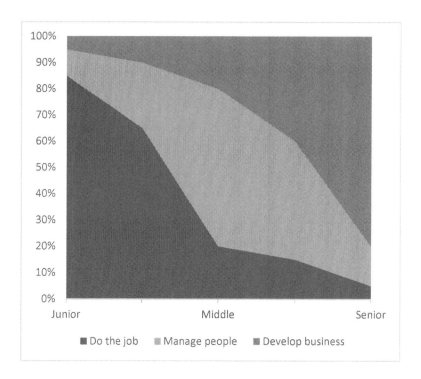

Skills mix graph

Success in your specialism is what will then tend to drive your early career progression into management.

As you rise within your job however the emphasis switches away from doing it as managing others doing it becomes a larger and larger part of the task (albeit that in order to supervise and train them you often have to keep your hand in to both keep your staff's respect and to understand developments in your sector or functional area and new ways of working).

As you become more senior in management your specialist technical skills then start to be less important (as technical tasks can always be delegated to specialists) and as a manager you will be judged on how well you manage people and your team to deliver the results required.

It's then your wider, softer skills in managing people and relationships which will become the key to further progression.

At very senior levels the role is increasingly focused on the development and direction of the business, where the task is no longer the day to day management of people and what is done now, but is about positioning the organisation and developing it and its networks and relationships so as to face the future, often described as *Working on the business rather than in it*.

So, you need to recognise how your role will change as you progress and plan ahead to be developing your skills and capabilities for the roles you want to advance to.

Every time you look at a new job or a project you should be asking yourself how it and the people involved are going to help you grow and develop your career. Because if they aren't, then shouldn't you be finding something else which will?

Just because you are good at something doesn't mean you need to keep on doing it. You need to find tasks and projects which will challenge you. Company fast track schemes will usually be deliberately designed to stretch participants both to test them, and as the fastest way of helping them learn and develop the skills they need to progress, so create your own personal fast track scheme.

Use success in these projects to create momentum, taking in more and more responsibility and being accountable for your success, and your failures, as yes, you will have knock backs which you will have to work through, but sometimes these are the things that teach you the most (and having had businesses fail, I've learned some pretty expensive lessons along the way).

Laying the foundations of your career

Even if you've no idea what you really want your career to be yet, it's never too early to start laying the foundations by way of developing a professional approach to the business of you, your professional persona and how you are seen.

Your personal branding starts now and you need to:

- **Know your dream, your story and have your personal sales pitch** – you need to be able to clearly tell people who you are, what you're about, and what you're looking to do with your life.

  You need to be someone with an ambition, a dream and a plan

to achieve it, even if at this stage it's about exploration rather than some determined direction, otherwise you are, and will look like, someone who's just drifting.

- **Dress for the job you want, not the one you've got** – appearances matter so I'd also add act appropriately for the job you want as well. You may have heard the expression *Fake it till you make it* which can be a dangerous approach if you are holding yourself out to have skills you don't have.

  But as *manners maketh the man* (or woman), give the impression you want to give by demonstrating attitude and aptitude and in developing the right professional approach. I think there's a lot to be said for actively looking to get into character in this way.

- **Have a hinterland** – you need a life outside work and you will need to cultivate the habit of managing a sensible work life balance right from the outset.

  Have interests and passions outside work, things that engage, motivate and develop you as not only will they help you stay sane, but they will also help you with work and your career as they can develop:

  o alternative or additional social networks

  o skills and responsibilities to complement those you develop at work; and

  o your persona and reputation at your workplace, as people like people who are enthusiastic about things and your passion will rub off into a positive reputation at work.

  Being active at sport can be very good for this. Being particularly cynical, taking up squash or golf can be good career moves in the right organisations as they can often give rise to excellent informal networking opportunities (or at very least the opportunity to get out of the office on client golf days as opposed to non-golfers who get to stay behind and answer the phones).

Critically, these days you also need to manage your online profile and social media presence as ways of communicating your personal brand:

- **LinkedIn account** – LinkedIn has been described as Facebook for grown-ups and is the world's leading professional networking website (if you want to link to me, please do – just search for Mark Blayney, press connect and use the 'we've done business together' option to be able to send me a request, and let me know you've read this book in your note).

  If you want to be a professional at anything then you should set up and work on your profile on LinkedIn as it will be a key tool for you in creating and managing your network of contacts.

  Treat your personal description as a personal website and think carefully about your description and what search terms you want to be found for.

- **Personal website** – you need to lay claim to your name online so you may want to register your own domain name and set up a personal website with your profile and the messages you want to put out to the world.

- **Other personal social media accounts** – outside work you are likely to already have a social media profile across a variety of sites such as Facebook, Twitter, Instagram, Pinterest or many others. Having these is fine but you'll need to think about how you manage them and what impact anything you post on these might have on your efforts to build a professional online image.

Following on from this point, the message is you then need to manage these resources professionally, so you should:

- **Look right** – ensure your professional profile always has an appropriate biography and professional looking photograph of you dressed in business clothes.

- **Comply** – Check your organisation's guidelines and policies about online conduct and always make sure you comply with them.

- **Behave professionally online** – as fairly or unfairly, you will be seen as representing your organisation with what you do or say reflecting on it.

- **Think about what you post** – assume everyone at work will see everything on any of your profiles, so make sure they see the right stuff. Post and update your feed with things you are interested in and are of relevance, and avoid controversy or inappropriate content or comment.

- **Be proactive** – follow and link to appropriate people and organisations to keep informed and join and participate in appropriate groups on topics that are of interest or relevance to you as these will help you grow your profile and network.

Building your support network and contact base

It's often said that *It's not what you know, it's who you know*. I think I'd amend that to: *It's who knows you*, as your network of contacts will be absolutely vital for developing your career.

So you should actively look to network:

- **internally within your organisation** – by showing an interest in company events, participating in and volunteering for projects which give you an opportunity to speak to people across different departments and up and down your organisation; as well as

- **externally** – by attending events and meeting people in other organisations with whom you interact.

Now, many people find networking and particularly networking events, aka a room full of strangers, akin to their worst nightmare as they are nervous about starting and managing a conversation.

There are some ways to mitigate this problem such as:

- If you are attending an event it's a good idea to look at the guest list in advance if this is possible. Use this to see who's going to be there and who you might want to talk to. You can even try doing some research by looking at their LinkedIn profiles or finding their biographies on their organisations' websites to find out more about them to act as the basis of a conversation.

- If you have colleagues at an event find out who they know and ask for an introduction to get you started.

- Remember, many other people at an event will be on their own, uncomfortable at having to try to start a conversation and desperate not to be left out, so just try approaching someone who is on their own. Nine times out of ten they will be grateful you did and eager to talk.

So in general, when at a networking event:

- Be prepared, do your research if appropriate, make sure you have business cards and be smartly dressed to make a good first impression.

- Find people to talk to and be confident enough to approach them.

- Be positive in your approach, introduce yourself properly by shaking hands and look people in the eye when you are talking to them.

- Take an interest in them as a person, not just as a job function or a potential client contact.

- And so following naturally on from this, ask open questions about why and how which encourage them to talk about themselves.

- Ask if there's anyone else at the event the person you are with thinks you should be speaking to, and if yes, see if they can introduce you.

- Follow up with everyone you meet by linking up on LinkedIn as a minimum, arranging to contact where appropriate, and saying thank you afterwards for any introductions or leads they have given you.

Remember that at a networking event you are there to make new contacts and strengthen your relationships with existing ones. You are not there to stand in a huddle with your close colleagues and gossip with them, however much safer it feels. At any event you should set yourself a target of say three new people to meet, or contacts you've not seen for a while to catch up with.

But fundamentally, at any event you are going to have to talk to people otherwise there's no point being there.

To manage a successful conversation you have to:

- **Start it** – which doesn't need to be anything particularly witty or stunning, it can just be something fairly general, hence so many conversations start about the weather, or basic, such as introducing yourself (which after all is only polite if you've not met before).

- **Keep it going** – refer back to the chapter on communication skills if necessary but a conversation should be a mutual interaction with both parties talking and listening, so remember to be an active listener, think about your non-verbal communication, and show an interest in the other person by asking questions such as about their interests, but without getting too personal.

  People generally like to talk about themselves if they have a sympathetic or interested listener so try to ask open-ended questions starting for example, with how or why, as these can easily lead into an explanation as an answer:

  - How did you come to be in this type of work?

  - Why do you like what you do?

  - What are the best bits about it?

  Depending on how it develops you might also disclose more personal information, such as interests outside work, or some vulnerabilities, as a way of building intimacy, however be careful about oversharing.

- **End it succesfully** – every conversation is going to end at some point, and in fact to make a success of an event by speaking to a number of people, you will need to end a number of conversations. Have a number of ways to end a conversation which you can use as appropriate. This can involve recognising that you are both there to circulate and make contacts but whatever reason for drawing a conversation to an end, make sure you have closed it off by exchanging contact deatils and where appropriate agreeing some follow up such as arranging a call or a meeting.

If you feel nervous about conversations of this type then you need to practise by making a deliberate effort to talk to people in everyday situations. These don't need to be lengthy conversations and could just be a few words of greeting or about the weather or a similarly innocuous subject with anyone from a stranger, someone serving you in a shop, or a colleague making coffee. The what and the who don't really matter, it's about acquiring the habit and confidence of opening an exchange.

To take yourself forward understand the environment you are in, or want to operate in

If you want to manage your career in an organisation then you need to think about what you need to do to meet that organisation's expectations and requirements, and be aware of the culture.

- Firstly, is there a career path? Some firms and roles will have little apparent scope for development and growth. Other types of employment can have very characteristic paths such as:

    o Professional service firms where there is typically an up and out culture as the business relies on recruiting large numbers of trainees who perform much of the day to day work while they gain their professional qualifications, and progression is on merit and performance. These are organised in the expectation on all sides that many or most of these trainees will then leave the firm after qualifying to develop their careers elsewhere, as there is not room for the whole cohort within the senior management positions.

    o Bureaucratic organisations have traditionally tended to have a buggins turn approach to promotion in which seniority and time served are seen as significant factors.

- Is there a fast track programme talent spotting for future leaders and looking to develop them? If so, how do you get on it?

- Is technical training and/or personal development seen as a high priority?

- Are any particular things seen as essential career building blocks (such as professional qualifications), key attributes required (an ability to sell and build a client following) or acknowledged pre-requisites for senior positions (an overseas secondment perhaps)?

- Is it a political organisation? Do you need a sponsor to succeed? If so, who should you choose and how do you get them to sponsor you?

Think of progressing at work as being a bit like a game or a competition. If you want to play you need to understand the rules, and the better you do, the better the chances of winning you have.

The characteristics and traits of exceptional employees

If you want to progress, whether in your current firm or in another, you need to develop a reputation as an exceptional employee. But what does this mean and what should you focus on?

There are some common themes in much writing about how to develop your career such as the importance of executive presence, gravitas, communication, and appearance, but these general terms can be difficult to translate into more specific attributes to work on.

However business magazine *Forbes* conducted a study to find out what makes employees successful. They interviewed 500 top business leaders to find out what set great employees apart and the leading factor chosen was personality (78%), compared to cultural fit (53%) and employee skills (39%).

And when it came to personality, this didn't mean exceptional employees necessarily had exceptional inherent personality traits, but simply that they used a combination of everyday emotional skills which almost anyone can look to develop and incorporate into their day to day working life.

As a result, exceptional employees were seen to have the ten following characteristics:

1   **Flexibility and a willingness to delay gratification** – they are the opposite of jobsworths and are willing to work on whatever's required regardless of what's in their job description. At the same time they look to do a good job, confident that rewards will follow rather than trying to negotiate these up front (so firms wishing to retain such employees need to recognise this and meet their reasonable expectations in due course).

2   **An ability to tolerate conflict** – they recognise that in any work situation some conflicts may arise and while they don't seek them or use conflict as a deliberate tactic themselves, they don't shy away from it when it occurs. They are prepared to stand their ground and present their position logically and calmly even when under personal attack.

3   **They can deal with difficult people** – allied to the above, they

are able to manage their emotions so as to deal with the frustrating and sometimes exhausting task of dealing with difficult people whether inside or outside of the business. They do so by approaching the situation rationally, being aware of their own emotions and keeping these in check to avoid letting the other person get to them and inflaming the situation with their own emotional response; whilst also trying to understand the other's viewpoint to seek common ground and build solutions.

4   **The ability to balance both focusing on a problem and managing ongoing requirements** – they have the knack of differentiating between real problems that require focus and action, and background noise; and they combine this with the ability to deal with the issue arising, while continuing to keep the day job's plates spinning.

5   **They are judiciously courageous** – as well as being willing to ask the difficult or embarrassingly simple question, they are also willing to speak truth to power when it's required and are not afraid to challenge a decision they believe is wrong; however, they do so to act constructively and not simply to be awkward, so they think before they speak and they choose their moments and the context in which to do so.

6   **They have an ego which is under control** – exceptional employees have egos which drive them to perform, but they also manage their ego so it does not get in the way of working with colleagues, and they are prepared to both admit mistakes and accept team decisions when required.

7   **They are dissatisfied with good enough** – they are committed to continuous improvement both personally and in respect of the business and they will always be looking for how things could be done better.

8   **They recognise problems as issues to be fixed, now** – and if they see a problem, they will want to address it immediately.

9   **They are accountable** – they own their own work and take responsibility for it. If it's good they will be pleased (subject to their ongoing thought that it could always be better if...); if there's been an error or mistake they don't hide it, instead they

look to address it with their manager so as to deal with any consequences and ensure it's right next time.

10   **They show leadership and marketability** – within the organisation they tend to be well liked and respected as a result of their integrity, and naturally display leadership even if not in formal leadership roles; while externally they represent the business's brand and values well and can be trusted to interact with clients and prospects.

So, if you want to be seen as an exceptional employee, it's never too early to start to develop some of these habits and approaches.

Training and skills – personal development and investing in yourself

One of the keys to continuing to develop your career is to ensure you are always continuing to learn, actively seeking out new skills as well as keeping up to date on your existing ones. I qualified as an accountant nearly 30 years ago but I would struggle to hold down a straightforward accounting focused job in industry or practice these days, as not only have both the regulation and technical elements moved on substantially since I took my exams, but the technology has too.

As it happens, accountancy like many professions, has a requirement for Continuing Professional Development (CPD or CPE for education) whereby to maintain my qualification I have to continue to study throughout my career. But what I have studied to help develop my skills has been focused on the work I am doing and want to do, so it has ranged across the subjects which are relevant to me such as marketing, lean manufacturing techniques, and even training in teaching and psychometric testing.

The world never stands still and neither should you. You should always be looking for chances to learn and develop new and relevant skills, whether it's through formal training, self-study or simply participating in new projects, mixing with new people from other backgrounds with different skills and approaches you can absorb.

You should always be working to keep yourself informed about the world around you, so if you don't already, start to read a proper newspaper. Even better, subscribe to and read *The Economist* as an essential weekly briefing on what is going on in the worlds of politics, technology, finance and business.

Finally, if you can find someone who can act in the role, see if you can find a mentor. It needs to be someone who:

- is experienced enough to help you navigate your way through work and life

- is happy to act as a sounding board for your questions; and crucially

- who you are comfortable speaking with so you can have an honest and open relationship.

For these reasons a mentor can't be your current boss as your working relationship can get in the way.

Deciding what you want to do

As I said at the outset, this chapter is not about career planning as such. This is such a huge subject and so important that you really do need to look at it seriously as a subject in its own right, so I'm only going to touch on it here in terms of how you should start to approach the subject.

As has hopefully already been made clear, if you want to have a successful career you need to:

- have a plan

- which you then implement.

But critical to having a plan to achieve success is understanding what success means for you.

In coming up with a plan you will need to take a clear look at yourself, your values and skills, and what you really want your life to be. So take your time and really think through some key questions you need to be asking yourself:

- **What do you really, really want to do?** – Some people already have a very clear idea about what they want to do with their life, others don't. If you're in the latter camp, try asking yourself: If money was no object, what would I do even if no one paid me to do it?

- **What sort of person do you want to become?** – What's your mental image of the person you would like to be? If it helps, think about people you know or have come across socially or seen at work who inspire you in any way. Is there anybody you can think of where you would say to yourself I'd like to be like them? In my case it was the company doctor.

- **What really motivates you?** – Different people are driven by desires for different things, to different degrees so if you are looking for a career which is going to satisfy you then you need to have a view on what will do it:

  o Rewards, money, wealth?

  o Power and authority?

  o Praise, recognition, status, or even fame?

  o Excitement, variety, pressure and challenge?

  o Security, stability, peace and quiet?

  o Relationships with the people around you?

  o Altruism and a feeling of having helped others, or the world?

  o Creativity and the chance to try new things?

- **What defines success?** – What levels of each of these are the recipe which is going to give you what you think you want?

- **What compromises are you willing to make to achieve what you want?** – I had always wanted to be a writer which I recognised was likely to be pretty precarious in terms of income, but I also wanted financial security. I made a choice early on to look to pursue a business career first, to try and get to the position of financial security where I could write full time (still working on it as you'll have gathered).

- **How do you like to work and how are you most effective?** – Are you someone who likes lots of structure or do you like to work independently? Do you enjoy company and a friendly collegiate office environment or would you thrive in a competitive environment where your performance is constantly being ranked against your colleagues?

- **What sort of physical environment do you thrive in, and what do you hate?** – This covers a wide range starting at its most basic with indoors or outdoors.

- **What are your personal skills and aptitudes?** – By this we're not just talking about whatever you might have specifically studied at school or university, although these are important, but more widely about your personal life skills, how outgoing you are, how analytic, how well you can build relationships and whether you are a good communicator. When you are looking to build a successful career it makes sense to play to your strengths as much as you can.

- **What do you want to be doing in five years, ten years?** – Having considered all of the above, then you need to create a personal vision, a picture in your mind's eye (or even better, written down and stuck up above your desk) of where you want to get to.

  And the more steps you can show by way of your plan of how to get there, the better.

Then, as we've already covered, you need to start to take responsibility for your own career development.

When I was starting out and came up with my plan to be a company doctor I wasn't explicitly thinking in these terms, but I did consciously think:

- **I wanted something that would be interesting** – I was already aware that I had a very low boredom threshold and enjoyed problem solving so I would need something which would give me variety.

- **Where I could have a high degree of independence, and ideally be my own boss** – as alongside my thirst for variety already went a strong streak of desire for self-reliance and an aversion for anyone telling me what to do; and

- **Where I could become rich** – I was very financially motivated already and even then had a personal ambition to be financially secure by the age of 50 (an ambition which I have miserably failed to achieve but hey ho).

- **At a job I felt I could do** – I had the arrogance to think if I worked at developing my career in the way I'd planned that I had the smarts and would develop the skills and experience to do this successfully.

And so, what I had seen of a company doctor in practice seemed as though it would suit me very well.

But what if things go wrong? Dealing with setbacks

Firstly, it's not a question of if things go wrong, it's when.

Over the course of your career you are going to have to deal with many, many setbacks and knocks, as I'm afraid that's just life. And if it's any consolation, it happens to everybody, not just you.

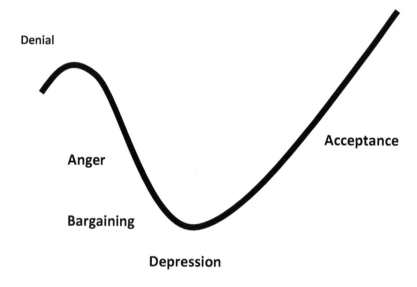

When something bad happens, we have a tendency to go through a number of emotions by which we come to terms with the problem which is known as the grief curve, developed by Elisabeth Kübler-Ross in relation to people experiencing bereavement. These are:

- **Denial** – in which we refuse to accept the problem.

- **Anger** – in which while we recognise the problem, we become frustrated and can lash out emotionally.

- **Bargaining** – in which we try to avoid the cause of the problem.

- **Depression** – in which we give up trying to avoid it as what's the point and we sometimes wallow in our misery.

- **Acceptance** – the final stage in which we accept the reality and face up to dealing with it.

So, if you've had a problem you shouldn't deny your feelings as you need to recognise and acknowledge your emotional reaction to the problem. However, you shouldn't let these emotional reactions overwhelm or define you either. You are a person with a wide range of attributes, you are not simply defined by the outcome of any particular piece of work, good or bad. If something goes wrong yes, take responsibility, but don't beat yourself up over it, and where necessary reach out to your support networks, at work or as appropriate, at home or socially.

Remember:

- **Don't take it personally** – stay balanced and remember that no one ever gets everything right all the time. Everyone, and I mean everyone, makes mistakes. Stay cheerful. Yes it's alright to be frustrated, but don't let it get to you, and start lashing out.

  Stay nice, figure out what went wrong and fix it and/or do it right next time.

- **A single setback does not equal absolute failure** – recognise that in life some things work out, and some things don't. You can never be right all the time so don't worry too much about the times when you're not. An individual problem is not usually a life changing disaster, so move on.

- **Learn from your mistakes** – errors and failures are valuable information that something does not work the way you thought it did, or some process or procedure has a weakness or a flaw which needs addressing. Don't waste a good problem. Always use it as a chance to improve.

  To grow you are always going to need to face challenges which take you out of your comfort zone and stretch you with things you've not yet done and may get wrong. It's called learning through trial and error after all. But it is all part of learning to get it right next time and setting your sights higher again.

- **Realise it won't last** – time moves on and what may seem dreadful now will soon pass.

- **Pick yourself up and try something new** – there's nothing like a new project to take your mind off a problem in an old one. So think big and pick a big new challenge.

In fact, some would counsel that you should actually love rejection and failures, and use them as the spur to drive you on.

I'm not sure I'd go that far, but certainly, you shouldn't let them hold you back.

9 Managing people and emotions

I'm an animal.

You're an animal.

We and everyone around us are animals, the product of millions of years of evolution, and let's face it, we're only 3% of our DNA away from being chimpanzees.

So what does this mean for how we behave?

Well as far as that fount of all authority Wikipedia tells me, current thinking is that our line of hominids evolved on the African plains, splitting off from the apes 5.6 to 7.5 million years ago, with species using fire and complex tools about 1.3 to 1.8 million years ago, and we've been Homo Sapiens for about 200,000 years. But it wasn't until about 15,000 years ago we began to develop agriculture; and the first city communities, with their need for us to develop complex social hierarchies, codes of conduct and social norms to make them work, then only emerged about 8,000 years ago.

So, when it comes to how we react and deal with a challenging situation there's:

- the deeply hard-wired, multi-million years of evolution honed, instinctive ways that enabled your ancestors to survive while sharing the savanna with lions; or

- the way we feel is socially acceptable given our modern social conditioning; or

- how we might think we ought to react logically.

When push comes to shove, I know which one I'd have my money on as the natural default way I, you, and everyone else will tend to react in the first instance.

But at the same time, because these are default natural reactions, people tend not to step back and question why they are reacting in certain ways and crucially, what they can do about it.

Understanding your drives, motives and needs

Obviously there is a large body of psychological and sociological research on why we do things and one of the fundamental sets of distinctions can be characterised as the difference between:

- **Drives** – innate with physiological bases which tend to be activated by deprivation (*I'm hungry*) and be aimed at satiation (*I need to eat*); and

- **Motives** – learned and have a social basis (you'll probably have strong opinions that feel perfectly natural to you as to whether it's OK or not OK to be polygamous, drink alcohol and eat beef, pork, or dog, but these will depend heavily on your cultural background).

Obviously in normal circumstances there is a degree of interaction between these. I'm hungry, but generally given my cultural background that doesn't mean your pet Fido is at risk. Although as will become apparent below, if the situation becomes really desperate such as in a city under siege, then things may well change.

American psychologist Abraham Harold Maslow ranked seven innate human **Needs** of which the first five operate as a hierarchy:

1   **Basic survival needs** – such as sunlight, food, water (and sex is often listed here as well).

2   **Safety needs** – principally freedom from threats such as the environment, animals or other people, through shelter, security, order, and predictability.

3   **Love and relationships** – for feelings of affection and belonging.

4   **Esteem and reputational needs** – for feeling valued, recognised and respected; and

5   **Self-actualisation** – for the ability to develop and be self-fulfilled.

The way this 'Hierarchy of Needs' works is that:

- Needs don't motivate you until the prior ones are satisfied (*If you are desperate for food then you'll risk the lions to go and find berries*).

- Once a need is satisfied it doesn't motivate you any more (*once you have eaten you'll be focused on making sure you are safe*).

- We have an innate desire to work our way up the list.

- And experience of self-fulfilling activity tends to generate an increasing desire for more so it is not self-satisfying in the way that having eaten sorts out hunger for a while.

People's emotions and their Reaction Compass

I won't go into a lot of the background detail and psychological underpinnings of this but Affect is the technical term for the experience of feeling or emotion.

Script Theory developed by Silvan Tomkins (which has then given rise to Restorative Practice, visit hullcentreforrestorativepractice.co.uk for more information) is a model in which there are reckoned to be nine main Affects. The theory suggests these Affects are hard-wired survival instincts which have evolved to ensure we act in ways which support us in meeting our basic survival and safety needs (and therefore pass them on to our descendants):

Positive – designed to motivate us towards maximising our experience of good things (like that bush full of nice berries):

- enjoyment/joy (reaction to success/impulse to share) – characterised by smiling, lips wide and out;

- interest/excitement (reaction to a new situation/impulse to attend) – characterised by eyebrows down, eyes tracking, eyes looking, closer listening.

Neutral – designed to make us sensitive to change (so that a lion can't sneak up behind us while we're eating those berries):

- surprise/startle (reaction to sudden change/resets impulses) – characterised by eyebrows up, eyes blinking.

Negative – designed to protect us by giving us appropriate reactions to minimise our experience of a range of threats/bad things:

- fear/terror (reaction to danger/impulse to run or hide– *Hell, Lion!*) – a frozen stare, a pale face, coldness, sweat, erect hair

- anger/rage (reaction to threat/impulse to attack – *Hey you! Those are my berries!*) – frowning, a clenched jaw, a red face

- disgust (reaction to bad taste/impulse to discard – *Ugh those berries are bad!*) – the lower lip raised and protruded, head forward and down

- dissmell (reaction to bad smell/impulse to avoid – similar to distaste – *Ugh those berries smell off*) – upper lip raised, head pulled back

- distress/anguish (reaction to loss/impulse to mourn) – crying, rhythmic sobbing, arched eyebrows, mouth lowered

- shame/humiliation (reaction to failure/impulse to review behaviour – *Yes I'm sorry, I stole the berries!*) – eyes lowered, the head down and averted, blushing.

OK but so what? you may well ask, since nowadays you generally don't need to be really worried about being eaten by a lion.

Well, just because you now work in an office doesn't mean that those old hard-wired evolved survival mechanisms have just gone away. Now they may be triggered by other modern-day things like stress, a tight deadline for the big boss, or a lack of control of who's giving you what work and so on.

The important thing in this model of behaviour however is what happens when a negative affect is triggered, which has a few different names but for the purposes of this book think of it as a person's **Reaction Compass.**

The idea of Script Theory is that when something bad or threatening happens (*Lion!*), as a survival trait so as to be able to react quickly, we have also evolved four hard-wired default programs of behaviour (scripts) which we all jump to and run automatically – whether it's actually appropriate or not (think of this as a slightly more sophisticated version of the fight or flight reaction).

These four automatic instinctive responses to a negative emotional stimulus are:

1 **Attack other** – go on the offensive in an aggressive way. *Hey, you having a go at me? Well let's just see about that, Buster!* There's nothing more effective to make you feel better sometimes than letting rip and having a go back (whether they were actually having a go in the first place or not). This sort of reaction involves shifting any feeling of blame back onto someone else; make them feel smaller through anything from teasing, sarcasm, insults and right up to anger and physical assaults, and it makes us feel bigger and higher status.

2   **Attack self** – or people can seek to defuse the threat by putting themselves down, belittling themselves and using self-deprecating humour, which can also shade off into passive aggressive responses. (*Well of course it's all my fault! It always is, isn't it?*) It's a bit like, well if I can't control the situation, at least I can control the condemnation by doing it myself. (*If I'm going Oh silly me, I'm useless at this, aren't I? then perhaps the nasty person will go away and stop telling me off.*) Of course, if the person telling you off is yourself then this really doesn't get you very far as a strategy.

3   **Withdrawal** – we can try to avoid the conflict by severing connection with the other people involved and their actions, scrutiny, judgment or whatever form the perceived threat takes by going quiet, breaking eye contact, and refusing to engage.

4   **Avoidance** – or we can react by diverting our own and other's attention away or by some form of displacement activity. I'm going to ignore this bad thing by either losing myself in drink or drugs to drown it out, or I'll just choose to focus on something I do really well which quite often leads to high risk (*Hey look at me*) behaviour.

And obviously, some of these reactions (such as attack other) can then create negative affects in other people pushing them onto their compasses as well so you can end up getting exchanges like:

- You perceive some adverse feedback (or say dumping work) as a criticism or a threat which creates a negative affect in you

- which pushes you onto your reaction compass, and if it happens automatically run your attack other programme

- as a result the other person now feels attacked, creating a negative affect in them

- which in turn also pushes them onto their reaction compass

- and if they run at attack other script as well

- then off you both go into a blazing row...

The key point of all of this is to recognise that:

- when faced with a threat in its widest sense, you, like everyone else, may default to one of these positions as a natural reaction

- but it is just a natural emotional evolution driven reaction, not involving any thought in deciding you feel that way – it's not who you are

- and as just an automatic emotional reaction, it may well not be the appropriate one for the circumstances

- but now you are aware of this process

- and so you don't have to be just controlled by your reactions

- you can choose to recognise – OK I've had that instinctive reaction, but now what is the rational part of my brain going to decide I should feel about this? What do I want out of this situation and what should I do?

Don't get me wrong – I know getting over some of these natural reactions particularly when they've become habituated ones can be bloody difficult and in odd cases, nigh on impossible (there are a couple of people I have had very stressful situations with over the years that I am on lifelong withdraw from). But I think you may be surprised by how often you might be able to look at how you react from the outside using this awareness, and then decide to do something about it better calculated to achieve what you then decide you actually want.

It's also VERY VERY important to realise that this process will be happening in everyone around you all the time, the difference being, they by and large haven't thought it through and so will tend to be driven by their instinctive compass reaction – AND they will tend to stay on this until something changes.

Remember this and I think it will help you to manage people both in work and other relationships.

Please note before we go any further, this isn't the only psychological model that's useful in the world of work, and later in this chapter we'll also look at transactional analysis.

Getting off the compass

So you can identify when someone else, or you, are on their compass? That may be all very interesting in understanding what's going on and driving behaviours but really, so what?

Well it would be so what if it didn't then give you an opportunity and some mechanisms with which to do something about it.

When someone is acting on their reaction compass what they are doing is an affect, emotionally, driven set of reactions running as an automatic programme.

If that someone is you, and you can recognise what is going on, then you can (with effort) often choose to step off your reaction compass to be able to take decisions and act in a rational way.

But that still leaves the other person who's decision-making and actions are still being run on the basis that they are being chased by a metaphorical lion, and they are therefore not in the best place to engage in rational discussion with you.

So what can you do?

What you want to do is get them off this automated programme and give their logical rational thought processes a chance to regain control.

Well, go back to the list of nine affects and you'll see this:

Neutral – designed to make us sensitive to change so that a lion can't sneak up behind us while we're eating those berries: surprise/startle (reaction to sudden change/resets impulses) – eyebrows up, eyes blinking.

The neutral affect is in effect a reset button, it flags there's something new so there is a need to switch out of the current state to take notice of.

With experience (and usually by using what's known as affective language, which is language which explicitly talks about how you feel), it can be used to break the hold of the programme their reaction compass is currently running.

As an example, imagine someone is being really angry towards you about something that's happened.

Your natural reactions (and therefore those they subconsciously will be expecting to deal with) are on your compass, attack other (fight back), avoid (run away or try to deny blame), attack self (abase yourself), or withdraw (clam up).

So what's their reaction if, for example, instead you calmly agree with them saying, *You're right to be upset. If that happened to me I'd be angry too.*

Is that going to take them by surprise? Unless it's happened before, in all likelihood, yes.

Is it going to take the wind out of their sails? Are they going to have a moment's confusion while they process what you've said? Probably (depending on how full blown the rant). Bear in mind, the more emotional the state, the bigger the surprise has to be to cut through it.

Is it going to jerk them out of the flow of their emotional angry response long enough and far enough for there to be a chance of them starting to deal with the issue more rationally? Hopefully.

If you do need to discuss the row later then I'd suggest you use some specific language. You don't want to start the row again so don't say anything that:

- is critical of the other person (or an attack which generates a negative affect); or

- has contestable facts.

Instead you again want to use affective language. So, compare and contrast these two sets of phrases:

1   ***You were unfair yesterday and upset me***

    This sort of statement can create a problem as:

    - It can be seen as an attack on them and so here we go back on their compass, and

    - It contains a contestable fact (giving them an opportunity to base an immediate attack other response: *No I wasn't, I was completely justified!*)

Versus

2   ***I was upset yesterday because I felt it was unfair***

    This is a much less problematic statement as it's about your feelings and so:

- It's not accusatory, it's a statement about how you felt about the situation.

- It's true and by its very nature not contestable – you own your feelings, so what can they say? *No, you weren't upset? No, you didn't feel it was unfair?*

A word about humour

Appropriate use of humour in a work environment can be a very effective way of both communicating and building bonds. It can also be used as a way to tackle difficult situations, but it is also often very risky as it can be interpreted as:

- a failure to treat work and/or a particular situation with the seriousness it deserves (particularly by an aggrieved party – *This is no joke you know*)

- insubordination (*Who do you think you are?*)

- a threat (*Are you taking the micky?*); or even

- passive aggressive behaviour.

So I would be very cautious about using humour as a way of responding to difficulties in any conflict situation until and unless you are very sure of the workplace culture and how this will be received.

You need to ask yourself how well would this go down in your organisation and from you in your position?

If you are already an accepted member of the team and seen to be really one of us and living and breathing the team's values, then humour could work well because you have passed these first tests it will be taken as a positive contribution.

If you haven't passed these tests and are still seen as an outsider or someone who still has to be proven, then humour could easily be taken as a sarcastic attack on how 'we' work and how you are being treated and is likely to be seen very negatively. So, a negative affect as a result of your attack, how do you think that's going to work out for you?

In other words, you always need to put yourself in the other party's shoes and think through how it will be seen by them.

The ethics of affective communication

Some people can feel uncomfortable about the idea of using affective communication.

For some this is for reasons we've already touched on in connection with assertiveness, that it feels too self-centred and focused on getting what you want out of interactions.

However, I'd argue this is simply about understanding the emotional impact of how you are interacting with other people, recognising how it can have a hugely adverse impact on how this goes (how constructive is it for anyone to be on their compass?) and being open and honest about your feelings.

For others there's a feeling this:

- is somehow a manipulative approach designed to give an unfair advantage; and/or

- it requires them to think about other people as objects or systems to be manipulated as though you are treating them as pawns in a game you are playing.

As a result, they see it as requiring a cold-blooded approach to understanding other people's emotional reactions, and using these to get the results you want.

Again, I'd argue this is simply a matter of recognising the emotional underpinnings of how we interact with each other and taking steps to avoid negative emotions to create barriers to understanding.

If there's one thing which I hope you will have picked up from this book so far, it's that you need to develop effective and respectful relationships with the people you work with. So to me, done properly and with that spirit in mind this just seems part of how to develop those types of relationship.

And I'd also suggest the reality is that you are playing a game all day, every day, every time you interact (note the word act) with anyone.

The choice is whether you play it unconsciously without noticing it and what you are doing, in which case you are trusting to luck and whatever habits you pick up as to how it plays out; or you can decide to become a conscious player and look to proactively manage how you play so as to have the best chances of getting what you want (and avoiding what you don't).

That doesn't have to be manipulative and in fact, in the longer term, it's a very difficult and energy sapping thing to try and do.

Don't overdo it. Be natural, recognise and respect your and other people's emotional reactions to what's happening or said, and use this knowledge as one of the tools in your kitbag to help you avoid adverse emotion driving decisions.

Transactional analysis and I'm OK, you're OK

Of course, the compass model described above is only one of many many psychological models developed over the years to help understand people and their reactions. I simply major on it here because I find it a particularly useful one in practise, however there are others which I'll also apply when it seems appropriate.

Of these probably the second set of tools I'd reach for by way of useful models and categorisations for assessing how people behave come from Transactional Analysis developed by Eric Berne after WW2 and described in his book *Games People Play*.

In the transactional analysis model people have three main sets of behaviours, thoughts and feelings, which have a pattern of positive and negative characteristics:

Role	Source	Subtype	+ve aspects	-ve aspects
Parent	Copied from parents or parent figures – what you saw people do	**Nurturing parent** Copying my parents looking after me	Genuine interest in person helped Protective Supporting Calming	Can be patronising
		Controlling parent Copying my parents telling me what to do	Genuine interest in person helped Directive	Critical Blaming

Role	Source	Subtype	+ve aspects	-ve aspects
Adult	Direct responses to the immediate environment		Reasonable Logical Unthreatened/ing	
Child	Learned behaviours replayed from childhood	**Free child** My behaviours without regard to what my parents say	Expressiveness Curiosity Creativity Spontaneity	Tantrums Rebellious-ness
		Adapted child Ways of behaving which fit into what my parents expect	Awareness of social needs	Dependency Insecurity Conformity

The transactional part of the name comes from considering how individuals operating in different boxes interact with individuals operating in other boxes.

Patterns of transactions which occur regularly (imagine for example what might happen when someone operating as controlling parent meets someone acting as adapted child and how the two are going to tend to interact) are known as games, hence Games People Play.

Additionally, Berne suggests there are four fundamental life views that an individual can hold which helps determine how they see the world and act towards others:

I'm OK You're Not OK	I'm OK You're OK
I feel good about myself but see others as damaged or less capable, can lead to unhealthy or even bullying behaviour in relationships as I see myself as the stronger partner	Positive state where I feel good both about myself and others and their competence, leads to self-confidence and fairness

I'm Not OK You're Not OK	I'm Not OK You're OK
The worst-case scenario where there is no hope since everyone is seen as being in as bad a state, leading to despair	I see myself as the weaker partner while everyone else is better off, leaving you vulnerable to accepting abuse

For a fuller exploration of what's summarised very briefly above read Eric Berne's *Games People Play*, and *I'm OK, You're OK* by Thomas Anthony Harris).

10 Managing stress (don't read this chapter)

After we'd both left a particular firm, one of my ex-colleagues used to joke that he lay awake at night, worrying his stress levels were too low, but in reality, stress as a problem is no laughing matter.

And so this is the chapter I hope you never have to really use; some words about stress.

Why you should not read this chapter

But before getting too far in, please recognise that stress is good. In moderation.

Stress is a normal, natural and even healthy long evolved reaction to a variety of circumstances. A degree of stress around an important project or event can be a spur to high achievement for example. Some people even seem to thrive on stress as it gives them the challenge they need to succeed.

In this sense occasional stress can actually be a good sign. After all, to learn and develop you need to challenge and stretch yourself by working outside your comfort zone, and one of the ways you know you are doing this is it's stressful.

But by managing through that stress and succeeding in whatever you were doing, whether it's standing up to do a presentation or juggling a heavy workload, you will build your confidence as you see you can do it, which will reduce the stress factor next time.

If you are finding some parts of work stressful that's actually probably fine and a natural part of what is going to be a steep learning curve; in which case I would seriously advise that you **DO NOT** read the rest of this chapter.

I say this, because this chapter is not about dealing with the occasional acute stress of the need to succeed.

Instead it's about those times when chronic stress becomes a problem.

Like many long evolved good and useful things, stress is something we can have too much of and find it challenging in modern life where excessive levels of continued stress can lead to a range of problems including sleep loss and behaviour problems, and can even trigger depression.

Two important notes

Firstly, the material in this chapter has been written from a mix of personal experience and professional material on dealing with normal levels of stress in the workplace. It is intended as a practical guide to help you understand and manage this as an issue in everyday life.

However, I'm not a doctor, therapist or health professional, and if you are suffering from levels of stress that are causing you concern, you should not rely on this material but should seek appropriate medical advice.

Secondly, one of the reasons for including this chapter is that from personal experience I'm a great believer in the value of knowing your enemy in terms of awareness and understanding what is happening and why, as the key first step in dealing with any problems.

But one of the dangers of raising awareness is that some readers may become more conscious of the symptoms noted in ways which could be stressful in themselves (*Oh no, this is happening to me and look how it could get worse*) so I would caution against allowing anything in this chapter to wind you up or increase your stress levels.

So again, before reading further:

- if you are just having occasional stressful periods around particularly challenging pieces of work – I suggest you don't read this chapter; and

- I would emphasise that if you feel you are having real problems in coping due to stress you should seek medical advice.

Stress's biological role

Going back to the idea of fight, flight or freeze, stress's basic biological role is as a survival mechanism to protect us from danger. (*It's that damn lion again.*)

Stress is a reaction which puts us on alert to a threat, keeps us there until the threat has passed, and using things like adrenaline induces temporary changes to our bodies to enable us to react in ways that make sense when dealing with that lion:

- **Vigilance** – improves as you stop ongoing normal activity and seek to focus on the source of danger (and this includes an elevated awareness of your own body, where the unfamiliar stress symptoms will be noted and can feed back into the stress feeling). So you will feel tense, wound up, and easily startled, while concentration on the everyday becomes difficult and your mind can go blank.

- **Anticipation** – your mind is then working overtime to work out how close and serious the threat is, how it might evolve and where it may threaten next. (*What if the lion goes that way? Can it then sneak up behind me? Is it on its own or is there another one?*) So you have an overall feeling of apprehension as you wait for something potentially very bad to happen. Ever had a feeling of constant dread for no adequately defined reason? This is it.

- **Circulation** – your legs and arms are going to need blood to be able to fight or run so it's moved from where it's not needed, so skin and extremities can become cold, pale, numb or tingling.

- **Breathing** – your body is going to need more oxygen to be able to run so breathing quickens and you can feel breathless, choking or dizzy.

- **Muscles** – tense for action so as to be able to hit or run, sometimes leading to shaking.

- **Sweating** – increases to cool those working muscles.

- **Pupils** – dilate to let in light and improve peripheral vision (*You don't want to miss that lion if it sneaks round the side*), can make you sensitive to light and even have spots in front of the eyes.

- **Digestion and salivation** – slow down as they're a waste of energy needed elsewhere so expect nausea, a dry mouth, and in extreme cases bladder and bowel problems – giving you something else to worry about!

And while these reactions come on very quickly so as to ready you for action, they are slow to diminish, again for very understandable evolutionary risk management reasons. While the lion is now out of sight, it might not have gone far, so it makes sense to stay on the alert and not let your guard down too soon. That feeling of tenseness will last for quite a while and you'll feel your body's reaction by way of tiredness afterwards as well.

Most of which is fine and can be coped with if the threat is an occasional lion that goes away again. But when the threat is today's workload and tomorrow's and the day after that, then we can have problems caused by this crisis orientated mechanism being stuck on a continual state of alert.

Given this it's easy to see why work, and especially a first job, can give rise to stress:

- New environment (*There may be metaphorical lions about*)

- Don't know the rules (*You don't know where the lions might be waiting*)

- No support network (*You don't know if others are keeping an eye out for lions and/or will warn you*)

- Lowest rung on the hierarchy (*You have low levels of control of what you are asked to do and therefore of your potential exposure to lions*).

Stress as a problem

People having problems with stress often:

- don't want to admit it as they fear it will be seen as a mental illness – it's not, (but if not dealt with properly it can get worse and affect your mental health, and your wellbeing through alcohol, drugs, poor diet and lifestyle choices);

- think others aren't affected by it – they are; or

- feel that they don't cope with it as well as others do – well people do vary in their susceptibility to stress and undoubtedly some are naturally better at dealing with it than others, but everyone can improve their ability to deal with it using established tools and techniques.

Things that can make you more susceptible to stress either generally, or at any particular point in time include:

- **Childhood** – a history of childhood insecurity such as bullying at school or uncontrollable events such as family breakdown, parental illness or death can leave people particularly vulnerable, as can having too much responsibility too young, perhaps as a carer, which can result in a strong desire to achieve, matched with deep feelings of guilt for any failures.

- **Modelling** – is the way we learn, in the first instance by copying our parents' ways of dealing with the world. On the positive side, it can be how we learn to deal with stress, but in negative cases such as having an anxious parent we can instead only learn that the world is a dangerous place while failing to be provided with coping skills and confidence.

- **Personality factors** – you may view yourself as a born worrier who can't cope with changes. No one however is actually born stressed or with the inability to cope with it. If you have become someone who is more prone to it, that's probably a learnt behaviour as a result of some of the factors listed above and it's equally possible to learn to deal with it better.

- **Perception** – problems in dealing with stress often come down to thought patterns and our learnt ways of responding to stressful situations. A tendency to respond to a stressful event by blaming yourself self-critically, focusing on all the potential negative outcomes and wanting to run away and hide is likely to reinforce, prolong and intensify a stressful response; whereas a more balanced view that yes, this is bad but I can manage, I'll get through it and things will be better afterwards, will tend to help you through and out of a stressed response.

- **Life events** – routine is usually good for a sense of security and safety (*No lions around here this week*) so anything that changes a routine can be a cause of stress. These can be negative events from the personal such as divorce, bereavement, injury, or other problems at home such as neighbourhood conflicts, crime or misbehaving children, through to work issues of conflict, overwork, long hours, a bad commute, underpay or that big conference presentation that's coming up. But equally, good things like getting married, having children, moving house, organising your holiday or taking retirement can also be stressful. Sometimes it doesn't have to be one extreme life event, as too many small changes over time can cause stress while often stressful events can be linked to each other (as a redundancy say, could lead to financial problems and then marital breakdown). Often people can bottle up stress so there is a time lag before the pressure cooker bursts and in these instances, it's often a case of the straw that breaks the camel's back as some relatively minor incident ends up being a trigger for the release of all that pent-up frustration.

How do you feel stress?

Stress is experienced in three ways summarised by the acronym TAB:

- **Thoughts** – what's going through your mind when you are under stress

- **Actions** – what you do and how you behave under stress; and

- **Bodily reactions** – the physical sensations you feel when under stress.

Thoughts

Thoughts typically include a range of negative or self-critical questioning and imaging such as I can't cope, I can't do anything right, people are looking at me, or negative imaging such as questioning and worrying about what if this or that goes wrong or mental imaging of it actually happening.

The underlying themes of many of these are fear, such as fears of loss of face and being criticised or made to look foolish, loss of control, rejection, loneliness; and on the other hand, of meeting people, and even illness (*I'm going mad*).

As a result, common problems experienced as a result of excessive stress can include difficulty in concentrating (*I need to keep an eye out for that lion*), irritability (attack other), sleep problems, an inability to shut off a stream of images and thoughts, incessant self-criticism (attack self), and negative imaging and collapsing self-confidence, or alternatively a loss of interest in the world and an increasing feeling of being shut off from it, disassociated or alienated, extending to feeling you are in a bubble shut off from the world or in some form of out of body experience.

These can then lead to typical avoiding behaviours of I can't face it, or them, I can't be bothered any more, or anxiety that I'm losing it, I'm going to faint or be sick, and at the extreme panic attack reactions (and these can be really scary and life changing, I've been there, done that).

Actions

Many of the typical actions experienced as a result of stress are, as described above, to do with avoidance so when suffering from excessive stress people will start to avoid normal day to day events which are perceived as contributing towards their stress levels such as socialising, talking to people, driving, or making decisions; and they may begin to act differently.

Life either starts to seem too hectic as they are unable to rest at peace, always rushing and speaking too fast or stammering while their performance and efficiency drops and they become accident prone and irritable.

Or, unable to cope, they may start to give up, shutting down, abdicating responsibility and avoiding people (sometimes in a hostile way) to be alone, which may be a warning sign for potential depression.

In either event they may seek escape through drink or drugs.

Bodily reactions

Finally, as I've tried to make clear at the outset, stress is a physiological state which has a long list of potential physical (and mental) symptoms that can be experienced, both:

- **Acutely** – with panic symptoms such as numbness, dry mouth, nausea, churning guts, shaking, faintness, heart racing, tightness of breath, jelly legs, disassociation, which can lead to full blown panic attacks, and the feeling of an overwhelming urge to escape.

- **Chronically** – with long term issues of sleep problems, tiredness, headaches etc.

Having looked at the biological function of stress at the start of this piece it is easy to see how and why the acute bodily symptoms of stress arise. They are in most cases simply the side effects of the natural stress reaction's survival functions.

The stress cycle

Given these three manifestations, you can probably already see the ways in which they can interact in a vicious cycle, feeding on each other to keep stress going.

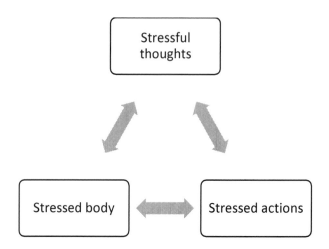

The stress feedback loops

Each aspect of stress, whether a thought, action or bodily feeling, can lead to one or more of the other signs (as that queasy feeling in your stomach – body – starts to make you worry – thought – and you begin to edge towards the door – action).

How do you deal with excess stress?

The secret to managing stress is therefore to:

- Recognise what it is and understand how it works from the description above.

- Face up to problems and avoid distractions.

- Break the cycle of stress (thoughts, actions and bodily reactions) by learning how to:

  o Tackle the immediate symptoms in the short term, and

  o Manage the longer-term symptoms.

Facing up to problems and avoiding distractions

Inevitably people do have real problems which cause real stress with which they have to deal.

Where there is a real problem (say there's a real-life lion-style threat to cope with such as a significant life event), then the issue is not just how to manage the stress. This may be of use in helping you to cope with the situation, but it's only dealing with the symptoms and not the cause.

If there is a real identifiable problem that needs to be dealt with, then this needs to be specifically addressed so as to tackle the cause of this particular stress at source.

Similarly, there may be factors which will hamper attempts to deal with stress such as a reliance on alcohol or drugs, or a desire for some kind of miracle magic cure, which will get in the way of taking the actual actions needed to address the situation. If any of these are in evidence they need to be dealt with to allow you to be able to take the steps which will actually help.

Managing stressful thoughts

How you think about a situation affects how you feel about it and unfortunately stressful thought processes and the way we talk to ourselves about how we are feeling and what it means tends to be unhelpful as they tend to be negative, unrealistic and self-reinforcing.

Stressful thoughts can often come out of the blue, whether we want them or not, and quickly build from some small issue (*The printer's not working*) on which you find yourself first focusing (*Oh hell that's going to make this report late*) and then generalising (*My IT never works*) and generalising again (*Nothing in my life ever works*) and off into a spiral of negative thoughts about how everyone else's life seems just peachy while yours has turned to crap.

This sort of unhelpful thinking style can involve a range of over generalised habits including:

- **Catastrophising** – always jumping to the worst possible conclusion, and then assuming it's the inevitable outcome; links to

- **Magnification** – being a drama queen in that any small thing is always a major disaster; and

- **Crystal ball gazing** – where you are able to look into the future, but only ever to foresee future disasters and problems.

- **Self-blame** – always seeing yourself as the cause of anything that goes wrong (even if there's no way in which it can possibly be your fault); and

- **Labelling** – always attaching negative and highly emotive derogatory descriptions to yourself and others as a matter of course; while

- **Emotional reasoning** – making the assumption that what you feel (*I'm a bad person*) is actually true; probably through

- **Continual reinforcement** – that sound track of negative thoughts that is on a continuous loop inside your head.

- **All or nothing thinking** – always seeing everything as black or white as say a complete disaster when everyone else always succeeds and there are no shades of grey; which is typical given

- **Unrealistic expectations** – where you have an exaggerated sense of what you should or ought to be able to expect; while

- **Disqualifying** – rejecting anything you recognise as good as being worthwhile; or

- **Minimising the positive** – regarding it as relatively small or unimportant compared to the problems you are focusing on; and

- **Overgeneralising** – allowing single negative events to colour your view of everything; while

- **Focusing negatively** – dwelling obsessively on a single thing that's gone wrong to the extent you refuse to see the things that have gone right.

If any (or all) of these seem familiar, then you need to look out for them in your own thinking next time you start to feel stressed and deal with them before they build.

The way to do this is to:

- **listen to your thoughts** and recognise them as valid; but then

- **challenge them**.

There are a few techniques for challenging your thoughts as they happen but the simplest is by always remembering to ask one or other of these questions:

- **What are the chances it could really happen?** – This question is useful when what you fear is actually very unlikely to happen. (*My heart is pounding; I'm feeling short of breath and I'm afraid I'm going to have a heart attack.*) Use logic and reference to actual data and experience to put things into perspective. (*I'm feeling really stressed and nervous about this big speech, but I'm actually quite healthy, I know I feel nervous like this with stage fright in this sort of situation, so the chances it's a real problem are slim.*)

- **What's the worst thing that could happen?** – This question is useful however when there's a reasonable chance your fear might come true but where the impact needs putting into a realistic context. (*What if I do X, or Y, or Z? Well would it really be the end of the world? It may seem a big thing here and now, but really, if you look back in five years' time is this incident really going to matter?*)

In the longer term it helps to develop a strategy to deal with stressful situations and the thoughts they will bring by:

- **Preparing for stress in advance** – if you can identify that something is going to be stressful then you can recognise that you will have a stress reaction and be prepared to recognise it, accept it as normal and deal with it. This may involve working out a plan in advance, and a conscious realisation that you are going to need to keep calm and to challenge negative thoughts with positive ones.

- **Facing up to it at the time** – part of your preparation may be to give yourself a script of questions to ask yourself like the ones above, or instructions to give yourself, *Remember to relax and practise my breathing techniques*, or statements to make to yourself such as, *I'm fine, this will pass and I know I can cope*, in order to challenge a cycle of negative thinking.

Work out a plan to deal with whatever the cause of stress is by applying a normal problem-solving process:

- o Identify and define as specifically as possible what the problem is.

- o Use this knowledge to help you compile a list of all the options you have to deal with this issue (don't be afraid to include doing nothing in your list as a specific course of action you may choose to take).

- o Work out the risks and pros and cons of each choice to allow you to choose the best option. (if it helps reuse the two questions above about what are the chances and what's the worst that could happen to help you think through each option and how they compare).

- o Turn this into an action plan; and

- o Do it!

- **Reviewing how it went afterwards** – and once you have got through a stressful situation you need to recognise the way you were able to actively manage your responses to deal with it and to celebrate your success as a way of building positive reinforcement for next time; while if it was still tough, well, what did you learn that can help next time?

Negative thoughts and patterns of thinking are inside your head. They're difficult things to shift but you do own them and if you want to manage stress they're something that you need to work to take control of.

As they say, you can't control everything that happens to you. But you do have choices about how you want to react to what does.

I have suffered from stress in the past, including full blown panic attacks, and one of the techniques I use is a sign I keep printed out on my desk at home where I can see it every day I'm working there. Using a very large font it fills a sheet of A4 and simply says:

- **Praise or silence** – this is an instruction to my inner voice that negative thoughts and running commentary are not allowed.

- **Everything in my world is changing all the time/there are always new opportunities** – this is to remind me that the one constant thing is change and it's to be welcomed, not feared.

- **My past is dead/I cannot change it so don't worry about it** – so no dwelling on past mistakes.

- **My time is finite/make the most of now** – enjoy the moment.

- **Look forward with hope** – be positive.

It helps me keep focused on what matters to me, so please feel free to use it and see if it helps you too.

Managing stressed actions

When you are stressed do you fidget or pace, or do you freeze? Do you talk nineteen to the dozen, or do you become tongue tied and stuttering? People act differently from normal when they are stressed. You may try and avoid the situation, switching off or depersonalising it as a way of avoiding responsibility or intimacy and exposure, or you may withdraw, seeking to escape the situation, or you may get aggressive, irritable and snappy with other people or yourself (is this reminding you of anything in the last chapter?).

Managing your actions when you are stressed is broadly a matter of seeing what stress is doing to your actions and consciously addressing them by:

- **Slowing down and taking control** – prioritising and choosing to focus on and clear one thing at a time. (Picking the worst thing and knocking that on the head first can be a great technique for getting you going, it's all downhill from there!)

- **Being realistic** – you aren't superman so divide problems up into manageable parts, build your team, confide in others and seek help when you need it.

- **Managing your time effectively** – To Do lists, routines and priorities (all of which help you generate a feeling that you are in control which reduces stress).

- **Looking after your relationships** – the people around you in your personal life and work life are a vital support network so make a conscious effort to ensure your stressed actions don't impact them.

- **Looking after your health** – through diet, exercise, sleep, and relaxation, and avoiding poor habits such as smoking, drugs, excess alcohol and excess caffeine.

To restate what's already been said above, some situations will be out of your control, but you own and can choose to control how you react to them.

Managing stressed bodily reactions

The opposite of stress is in essence relaxation (*No lions here so I can chill out*). Dealing with stressed bodily reactions is in essence about learning relaxation techniques, both:

- **short term techniques** – for dealing with the immediate acute impacts of stress; and

- **long term methods** – of reducing chronic stress levels and issues such as sleep.

Techniques that you can use to take control and deal with immediate symptoms of stress include:

- **Self-distraction** – diverting your attention away from the cause of the stress for a long enough period (usually a few minutes) so as to allow yourself to calm down:
  - focus on your surroundings or a specific object, ask yourself what you can see, hear, feel or smell
  - have positive mantras you can say to yourself when you feel stressed as an antidote, providing alternative message to the negative cycles of thought typical of stress
  - use a mental game or exercise that you need to concentrate on
  - concentrate on positive memories and images (so what would you do if you won the lottery?).

- **Breath control** – one of the feelings that people are most conscious of in stressful situations are changes in how they breathe which can lead to hyperventilating in extreme situations. So, learning how to bring your breathing back under control through taking long slow deep breaths in, holding them and then slowly exhaling can be very useful in getting your reactions back in control (as well as being a distraction technique in its own right as something to focus on).

- **Sharing** – get support by simply vocalising the issue can help you get a better perspective on it (even just writing down thoughts for yourself can often achieve the same effect).

Longer term steps are:

- **Exercise** – the old sayings about *healthy body, healthy mind* really do seem to have something to them, so start to get active; regular daily walks is a good place to start.

- **Relaxation** – learning effective techniques such as progressive muscular relaxation. Try searching YouTube for a range of meditation videos.

One of the key problems people suffer as a result of stress are sleeping difficulties. Not all sleep problems are stress related but stress can lead to issues in everything from getting off to sleep, to staying asleep, to getting up again.

Treating sleep problems is worth a book on its own (and indeed there are many good ones out there you can get if you are having sleep problems) but the treatment in general involves:

- **Sleep diary** – understanding the problem by recording the problem, times and issues over a period.

- **Sleep hygiene** – taking the steps just to make sleeping easier and more natural through learning relaxation and calming techniques to get you ready for sleep and ensuring you have a restful environment in which to do so (thinking about your bedroom, its temperature, darkness and noise levels, your bed and so on).

- **Sleep retraining** – if this approach to improving your sleep doesn't work then a more major intervention in terms of retraining your body into a positive sleeping pattern may be required to create and instil a new set of sleeping habits. This approach will take time and persistence over many weeks if not months, as you need to break your old deeply ingrained habits and create new ones.

The basic approach used is:

- o you need to accept your bedroom is only for sleeping in (no reading or watching TV),

- o so you don't enter it to go to bed until you feel sleepy, but
- o if you don't fall asleep within 20 minutes then you're not sleepy enough, so get up and don't come back until you are
- o get up early at a regular time every morning (no excuses, no lie ins) and never try to catch up on sleep
- o repeat for as long as necessary.

Key points summary

In the introduction I mentioned three essential points which I hoped you would take away from this book.

By way of a summary I repeat these below, together with some key supporting points which will help you to achieve them:

1   Don't just work in your job, work on it.

- Take responsibility for managing yourself from the start

- Treat your new job as a learning opportunity from the outset

- Work out what you really want to do, and what you need to do to get there

- Develop the Business Plan for successfully developing product You

- Develop your personal sales collateral – your career aspiration pitch, and your appropriate social media presence

- Network

2   Work on having successful, respectful relationships with people

- Understand your organisation's culture, ethos and standards, and ensure you fit with them

- Understand yourself and your preferences – try taking psychometric tests

- Work on your listening skills

- Realise that people differ; work to understand their needs and preferred ways of working and communicating

- Understand different ways of dealing with people and develop your negotiation skills

- Learn to say No effectively – if you lack assertiveness, get training

- Understand your own and other people's emotional reactions, and how to deal with emotions including conflict within the workplace – use effective language

- Don't burnout, establish boundaries and an appropriate work/life balance, have a hinterland of interests outside work

3   Find out what your boss really wants, and give it to them

- Your boss is your customer for the work you do, treat them as such

- Understand what motivates your boss, their priorities, and their management style

- Invest your time in supporting others and working to make them look good

- Organise yourself and your work to be effective – practice 5S and develop strong time management

- Ensure you have strong communication skills and produce the highest quality output that you can

Manage to achieve the above and I believe you will be setting the foundations for a successful and fulfilling career.

Afterword

And that's it, almost.

Because now, I have a work project for you.

Draw up your SMART plan of what you want to do.

Then go out and do it.

And please do let me know how you've got on. Link to me on LinkedIn (search for Mark Blayney), and do join my dedicated LinkedIn networking group (www.linkedin.com/groups/13503031) First Job Readers to swap stories, hints and tips.

And if you've enjoyed this book, or even better, found it useful, please also do me two favours:

1   leave me a review on Amazon, Goodreads or other book review sites, and,

2   spread the work to your friends and colleagues via recommendations and social media.

In particular, if you think this book would really help anyone you know, please tell them about it – as a suggestion: try photocopying the contents page and giving it to them.

Many thanks in advance for doing all or any of the above as I'd appreciate it very much, and it only remains for me to say good luck and all the best with your career, wherever you take it.

Regards

Mark Blayney

Further reading and resources

Further reading

While I've made reference to a number of books and websites in this guide, to enable me to keep suggestions up to date I have set up a further reading and resources page on my website: www.theworkpress.com.

Workbooks and resources

I'm of an age where I still use dead trees for work purposes. On a day to day basis I manage my time using an approach to calls, To do lists, prioritisation, and project management that has served me so well over the years that I set up bound versions in Amazon a while ago for convenience so that I could buy the formats I wanted in a workbook form.

If you would like to use the same approach, these are available on Amazon:

A structured approach to daily time and project management

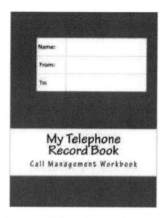

A telephone call logging and control book

I have also written a number of books for owner managers on business finance and creating and realising business value.

If you are interested in gaining an overview of what drives business finance and strategy some of these could be a good introduction so please visit http://theworkpress.com/business_books.html for more details.

27621604R00114

Printed in Great Britain
by Amazon